AMARNA

Ancient Egypt's Age of Revolution

For my granddaughter Alice
and my nephew Andrew Whitehurst

AMARNA

Ancient Egypt's Age of Revolution

Barbara Watterson

TEMPUS

First published 1999

PUBLISHED IN THE UNITED KINGDOM BY:

Tempus Publishing Ltd
The Mill, Brimscombe Port
Stroud, Gloucestershire GL5 2QG

PUBLISHED IN THE UNITED STATES OF AMERICA BY:

Tempus Publishing Inc.
2A Cumberland Street
Charleston, SC 29401

Tempus books are available in France, Germany and Belgium
from the following addresses:

Tempus Publishing Group	Tempus Publishing Group	Tempus Publishing Group
21 Avenue de la République	Gustav-Adolf-Straße 3	Place de L'Alma 4/5
37300 Joué-lès-Tours	99084 Erfurt	1200 Brussels
FRANCE	GERMANY	BELGIUM

British Library Cataloguing in Publication Data.
A catalogue record for this book is available from the British Library.

ISBN 0 7524 1438 0

Typesetting and origination by Tempus Publishing.
PRINTED AND BOUND IN GREAT BRITAIN.

4

Contents

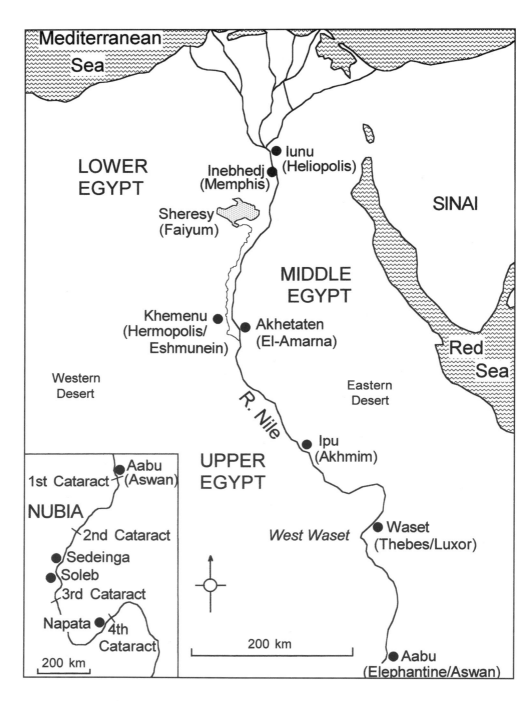

Frontispiece map of Egypt

Acknowledgements

I would like to thank my husband, Juan, for drawing the maps, the site plan and the genealogical table; and for his constant encouragement and support.

The site plan of Tell el-Amarna is based on a plan drawn for me by Professor H.W. Fairman in 1974.

The text photographs numbered **2, 9, 10, 20** and **28** are reproduced by kind permission of the Trustees of the British Museum.

The text photograph numbered **50** is reproduced by courtesy of Birmingham Library Services.

The photographs from the Ägyptisches Museum, Berlin, and the text photograph numbered **37** were given to me by the late Mr J. R. Channing.

All other photographs are my own.

Dynasty XVIII 1550 — 1295 BC

King (Prenomen and Nomen)

Nebpehtyre Ahmose (Amosis)	1550-1525
Djeserkare Amenhotep (Amenophis I)	1525-1504
Akheperkare Thutmose (Tuthmosis I)	1504-1492
Akheperenre Thutmose (Tuthmosis II)	1492-1479
Maatkare Hatshepsut	1479-1457
Menkheperre Thutmose (Tuthmosis III)	1479-1425
Akheperure Amenhotep (Amenophis II)	1427-1393
Menkheperure Thutmose (Tuthmosis IV)	1392-1383
Nebmare Amenhotep (Amenophis III)	1383-1345
Neferkheperure Amenhotep (Akhenaten)	1353-1337
Ankhkheperure Smenkhkare	1338-1336
Nebkheperure Tutankhamun	1336-1327
Kheperkheperure Ay	1327-1323
Djeserkheperure Horemheb	1323-1295

Note 1: The names in brackets are the Greek versions of ancient Egyptian royal names. In many books Greek versions are used in preference to the Egyptian because they were the forms found in Manetho (*see* Glossary).

Note 2: The ancient Egyptians did not themselves define years from a chronologically fixed starting point; thus no two modern authorities agree on the dates of ancient Egyptian history. The dates given above are based on those agreed on in P. Åström, ed., *High, Middle or Low?* Acts of an International Colloquium on Absolute Chronology Held at the University of Gothenburg 20-22 August 1987.

Glossary

canopic jars	jars containing embalmed viscera. There were four, each under the protection of one of the Four Sons of Horus: the man-headed god, Imset; the baboon-headed Haapy; the jackal-headed Duamutef and the hawk-headed Qebehsenuf. Imset, aided by the goddess Isis, guarded the jar containing the liver; Haapy, aided by Nephthys, guarded the jar containing the lungs; Duamutef and Neit guarded the stomach; and Qebehsenuf and Serket the intestines.
cartouche	ornamental oblong shape representing a loop of rope knotted at the base. Derived from the hieroglyphic sign meaning 'to encircle'. Two of the names which comprised the royal titulary (*see* below) were written inside a *cartouche* to signify that the king ruled over everything that the sun encircled.
Dynasty	*see* under Manetho.
Golden Horus Name	*see* under titulary.
hieratic	cursive form of hieroglyphs (*see* below). The word is derived from the Greek *hieratikos* (priestly).
hieroglyphs	picture-writing of ancient Egypt. The word is derived from the Greek *hieros* (sacred) *glupho* (sculptures).
ḥrp-baton	a wand of office; derived from an ancient Egyptian word meaning 'to control' or 'to administer'.
Manetho	Egyptian scholar-priest of the third century BC who first divided the kings of ancient Egypt into 30 groups known as Dynasties.
memorial temple	temple dedicated to the worship of a dead king.
mortuary temple	*see* memorial temple.
necropolis	cemetery; literally 'city of the dead' from the Greek *nekros* (corpse) *polis* (city).
nomen	*see* under titulary.
obelisk	shaft of stone (usually granite) with pyramid-shaped top; from Greek *obeliskoi* (little [roasting] spits).
prenomen	*see* under titulary.
rishi coffin	coffin that is anthropoid in shape, with a lid decorated with a huge pair of wings stretching from shoulders to feet as though enfolding the coffin. The wings represent those of

	the protectress goddesses, Isis and Nephthys. The modern name for this type of coffin is derived from the Arabic word for feather (*rishi*).
sarcophagus	stone coffin, from Greek *sarco* (flesh) *phag* (eat, swallow); literally 'flesh-eater' because of the custom during certain periods of Greek history to cover bodies within stone coffins with quicklime.
shabti	statuette placed in the tomb to perform tasks that the deceased may be required to undertake in the Afterlife; derived from the ancient Egyptian verb, *usheb*, 'to answer'.
sistrum, plural: sistra	strip of metal bent into a loop, the ends of which were bound together to form a handle. Rods stretched across the loop were strung with metal beads so that the sistrum, when shaken, rattled.
stele (or stela), plural: stelae	slab of stone, usually rectangular in shape with a curved top, decorated with relief and inscription.
Throne Name	see under titulary.
titulary	the royal titulary was made up of five names: the Horus name, which identified a king with the god Horus, of whom he was the earthly manifestation; the Golden Horus name, which may originally have identified the king with the god Seth although later, because Horus and Seth were regarded as mortal enemies, the Seth element was dropped; the *nebty* or Two Ladies name, the two ladies in question being Wadjet, the cobra goddess of Lower Egypt, and Nekhbet, the vulture goddess of Upper Egypt. The last two names in the royal titulary were *n-sw-bit*, meaning 'he who belongs to (*n*) the sedge (*sw*) and the bee (*bit*)', in effect, King of Upper (signified by the sedge-plant) and Lower Egypt (signified by the bee); and the Son of (the sun god) Re name, which was that borne by a king before his accession, and was almost equivalent to a family name. The *n-sw-bit* name is the prenomen or Throne Name; the Son of Re name the nomen: both were written inside a *cartouche*.
Uraeus	the goddess, Wadjet, worn in the form of an enraged cobra as the decoration on the front of a king's crown from which she was supposed to spit fire against the king's enemies. Word derived from the Greek, *ouraios* (snake).
ushabti	see under *shabti*.
wadi	Arabic word meaning dry river-bed.

Text figures

Text Photographs   *Page no.*

Colour plates

Preface

On the east bank of the Nile some 180 miles (300 km) south of Cairo, high desert cliffs sweep back to form a great embayment, a level plain between the desert and the river where sand drifts over the mud-brick ruins of the city known to the ancient Egyptians as Akhetaten (The Horizon of the Aten). About 250 years ago, a tribe of beduin, the Beni Amran, set up camp there; and the Danish traveller, Frederik Norden (1708–1742), who visited the district in 1738, noted that the area was called in Arabic 'Amrane' or 'Omarne' ('belonging to the Amran'), words which gradually evolved into 'Amarna'. The name of a local village, Et-Til, was corrupted to 'Tell', a word that normally refers to a large mound formed from the accumulation of rubbish on a long-settled site; and although there is nothing resembling such a mound in the area, Tell was added to Amarna to make up the modern name for Akhetaten, Tell el-Amarna. Akhetaten was inhabited for only a few years, but those few years are now known as the Amarna Age, an era of religious and artistic revolution.

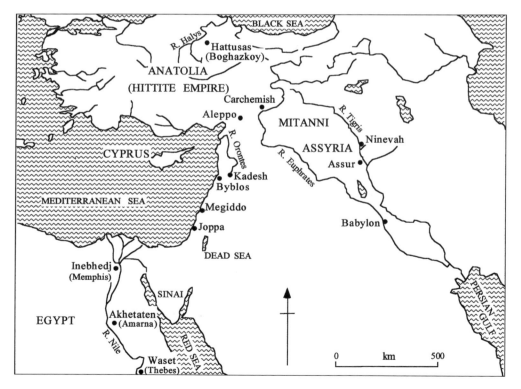

Fig. 1. Map of the Near East in the Eighteenth Dynasty

Introduction

Background to the Amarna Age: The Foundation of the Egyptian Empire

About 3100BC, the prehistoric chiefdoms and petty kingdoms of the Nile valley from modern-day Aswan to the Mediterranean were united under the rule of a single powerful king. Thus ancient Egyptian history began. For the next fifteen hundred years or so, the Egyptians lived securely within natural borders of sea and desert, unthreatened by outside forces and, apart from a brief period at the beginning, when Mesopotamian culture made a mark on Egyptian art, architecture and writing, impervious to foreign influences.

The rich natural resources of their land enabled the Egyptians to develop a unique civilization in which the king, regarded as a living god, was the linchpin of society. Major achievements in art and architecture were made in order to develop what was considered to be the focal point of the cult of divine kingship, the royal tomb, which from about 2660BC to 1600BC was a pyramid. A pyramid linked the king with the sun god, Re, who was the state god of Egypt, head of a pantheon of several hundred deities.

The royal succession was normally from father to son, although the fact that this sometimes did not happen is reflected in the way in which Manetho (*see* Glossary) divided Egyptian history into dynasties of kings. In the Thirteenth Dynasty (1786–c.1633BC), however, the crown seems to have changed hands frequently and never from father to son, indicating, perhaps, that there was an elective kingship. This led to the city of Sakha[1] in the north-western Delta seceding and forming the Fourteenth Dynasty (1786–c.1603BC). Although throughout most of Egypt the power of a single, central government continued to be respected for some time, it was inevitable that the instability of the royal succession would eventually have a detrimental effect on the stability of the country.

In the Twelfth Dynasty (1963–1786BC), beduin tribes known to the Egyptians as Aamu had been welcome visitors in the administrative district of Middle Egypt known as the Oryx, whose governor was responsible for large areas of the Eastern Desert whence they came; and in the tomb of Governor Khnumhotep at Beni Hassan male and female Aamu are depicted, some of them bringing gazelles as gifts. During the last years of the Thirteenth Dynasty, groups of people began to infiltrate into Egypt via the eastern Delta. The Egyptians assumed that they were either Aamu or the beduin tribes which had harassed the eastern border for centuries — the so-called Shasu (literally, 'sand-dwellers'). They were mistaken; and the new groups of people were making their way into Egypt with the intention of settling there.

The rulers of the Thirteenth Dynasty were too weak to prevent these migrants moving into the eastern Delta; and thus the Hyksos arrived in Egypt. The term Hyksos is Greek, derived from the ancient Egyptian *ḥḳȝw ḫȝswt* — 'rulers of foreign lands'. Where these foreign lands were is not certain but they are thought to have been east of the Caucasus Mountains. The Hyksos were made up of several western Asiatic peoples, although most were either Semites or an Aryan people known as the Hurrians; and over a few centuries they moved down into the Fertile Crescent, dislodging the sedentary peoples they encountered. Eventually, some of the incomers — the Kassites, who are thought to have originated in the Zagros Mountains in Iran — settled in Mesopotamia. Others, the Hyksos, who on the evidence of their proper names were largely Semitic, settled in Egypt.

The main Hyksos group took over the ancient capital city of Egypt, Inebhedj,[2] and ruled over most of Lower Egypt and the Delta as the Fifteenth Dynasty (1648–1540BC). A secondary group, the Sixteenth Dynasty (1648–1587BC), ruled over the north-eastern Delta. Sakha (Xois) survived as an independent city-state for forty years; and the native kings of the Thirteenth Dynasty continued to rule Upper Egypt until they were superseded by the Seventeenth Dynasty (c.1648–1550BC). The Hyksos regime in the north appears not to have been unduly harsh, and although they levied tribute from Upper Egypt they seem to have been on reasonably good terms with its rulers.

The Hyksos borrowed extensively from Egyptian culture: the names of their kings were written in hieroglyphs; and they either usurped the statues of former rulers or had copies made of them. They also had copies made of noted scientific and literary works, several of which — the Rhind Mathematical Papyrus and the Edwin Smith Surgical Papyrus, for example — survive today as the only known versions. In return, the Hyksos seem to have introduced the Egyptians to cultural innovations such as the vertical loom and the lyre, and to the use of the horse-drawn chariot, the composite bow and other advanced military equipment; so that the period was not the unmitigated disaster that native historians of later generations represented it.

Eventually, the native rulers of the Seventeenth Dynasty (*see* above) were able to drive out the Hyksos — ironically, using horses and chariots obtained from the Hyksos — and establish control over the whole land. Egypt, however, had been changed forever. For the first time in their history, the Egyptians had been conquered by foreigners and shaken out of their sense of security. They had for generations been confident that they were the chosen people of the gods, but the invasion by barbarians who 'ruled without Re' had brought home to them the realization that their country was not inviolable. The Asiatic Hyksos brought Egypt into contact with western Asia as never before; and thanks to them the Egyptians were provided not only with the military means to prosecute expansionary wars but also with the incentive. The early kings of the Eighteenth Dynasty determined to prevent any further influx of migratory peoples by setting up a buffer state between Egypt and western Asia; and to establish Egypt as the dominant international power. Accordingly, they initiated a policy whereby, first through war and then by diplomacy, they colonized their southern neighbour, Nubia, and established protectorates in western Asia, thus forming a great empire under Egypt's sovereignty.

Ahmose (1550–1525BC), son and brother of the last two rulers of the Seventeenth Dynasty, and founder of the Eighteenth (1550–1295BC), made the restoration of Egypt to the Egyptians his priority. His son and successor, Amenhotep I (1525–1504BC), stated that he was ambitious to 'extend the boundaries' of his country. Although his known military conquests were achieved only beyond Egypt's southern border, in Nubia, the fact that early in the following reign the Egyptians were able to penetrate deep into western Asia suggests that Amenhotep I had laid the foundations for such a move, enabling his successor, Thutmose I (1504–1492BC), to become the first of the great warrior kings who distinguished the Eighteenth Dynasty.

By the reign of Thutmose I, there had been a radical change in army policy. In the centuries before the Hyksos period there had been no need for a standing army, since there were no serious threats to Egypt beyond its borders. It had been necessary, occasionally, to mount brief punitive forays into western Asia, but otherwise troops were employed on quarrying and trading expeditions; and it was the responsibility of local governors to raise recruits as and when needed. From about 1900 BC, Egyptian interests in Nubia necessitated an efficient body of troops being permanently stationed there, but in Egypt itself there does not seem to have been a professional military class.

In the Eighteenth Dynasty, the Egyptian army developed, on a national basis, into a well-organized service in which military officers were professional soldiers rather than nobles co-opted *ad hoc*. Although officers were usually recruited from men of standing, uneducated men of ability were often able to work their way up through the ranks. The main body of the army was recruited by conscription; and training, which seems to have consisted of drill practice combined with physical punishment, was carried out in special camps. For the first time, the army included both infantry and chariotry, with the chariotry,[3] the élite corps, being equipped with the type of horse-drawn vehicles that had been used against the Egyptians by the Hyksos. The army was divided into three or four divisions, each of about 5000 men under the control of a general, usually one of the King's sons. The commander-in-chief was, of course, the King himself. There were 20 companies to a division, and every company normally had five platoons, with 50 infantrymen in each. In addition, there was the navy, which was employed primarily in the transportation of troops and equipment.

At the beginning of the Eighteenth Dynasty, the Syria-Palestine area to the north-east of Egypt consisted of petty princedoms and city states with no cohesion, and ripe, therefore, for conquest. By the second year of his reign, Thutmose I was able to state in an inscription engraved on a rock opposite the island of Tombos, south of the Third Cataract, that the northern boundary of his empire was set at the river Euphrates. The area between the Euphrates and the Tigris was the Kingdom of Mitanni, established by the Hurrians (*see* p.16), in about 1500BC. Mitanni was powerful; nevertheless Thutmose I managed to penetrate across the Euphrates into Naharin, the 'River-country', where a great slaughter was made and many prisoners taken.[4] Mitanni flourished for only a century or so, but during that time it was Egypt's greatest enemy, and was able to treat Assyria as a vassal state. Mitanni was finally to succumb to the growing power of the Hittites, who began to extend their influence beyond the borders of their homeland in central Anatolia; and by about 1350BC, Assyria, under the rule of King Ashuruballit, was able to regain its independence.

In 1492BC, Thutmose II, son of Thutmose I and one of his minor wives, came to the throne. His queen was his half-sister, Hatshepsut, by whom he had a daughter; but the son who succeeded him was the child of a royal concubine. The new king, Thutmose III (1479–1425BC), was still a child, and imperial ambitions were set aside when his stepmother, Hatshepsut, who acted as regent for two years before declaring herself Female King of Egypt, initiated an era of peace which lasted until her death some two decades later. Hatshepsut (1479–1457BC) left the country prosperous and well-organized, enabling the adult Thutmose III, by this time commander-in-chief of the Egyptian army, to lose no time in marching into Syria-Palestine to meet the growing threat from Mitanni.

A year before Hatshepsut's death, Mitanni had begun to supply men and equipment to a confederation of western Asian city-states, led by the ruler of Kadesh,[5] a city on the river Orontes in Syria. Thutmose III aimed to capture Kadesh, but first he had to secure a bridge head in Palestine. During his first campaign he captured the key city of Megiddo,[6] from which the Egyptians took an enormous quantity of spoil, and three other cities to its north, which were given to the Temple of Amun (*see* p.20). Meanwhile, one of his generals, Djehuty, had captured Joppa (modern Tel Aviv-Yafo/Jaffa) by smuggling his men into the city inside baskets in the manner of Ali Baba and his jars.[7] At the conclusion of this first campaign, Thutmose returned to Egypt to celebrate his victory in the Temple of Amun.

Over the next few years, the conquered rulers of Palestine and southern Syria sent much tribute to Egypt. In his fifth campaign (1451BC), Thutmose established land bases in Phoenicia, capturing several ports and a number of Phoenician ships, and in 1450BC, he sailed up the Phoenician coast to the port of Simyra, and thence to Kadesh, which he overthrew. In 1447BC, Thutmose fought the eighth and greatest of his campaigns. He sailed to Byblos and marched through the Lebanese mountains to the Orontes valley, taking with him boats on carts which were dragged overland by oxen. Having defeated the King of Mitanni at Aleppo, Thutmose pursued the Mitannian army across the Euphrates, and then sailed with his troops up and down the river in boats that had been dragged from Byblos via Aleppo, a journey of over 240 miles (400km).

Although settlements on the banks of the Euphrates were attacked, Thutmose made no attempt to invade Mitanni. The country was, however, cut off from its Syrian allies, encouraging other powers, notably the Hittites of Anatolia, to move against it. Such was the renown that Thutmose III brought to Egypt that in 1447BC Babylon and Assyria sent him presents, the Hittites sent silver and Cyprus a large amount of lead and copper. The seventeen campaigns[8] that Thutmose III mounted over the 32 years between 1457 and 1425 BC established an Egyptian empire in large areas of western Asia and made him the greatest warrior of all ancient Egyptian kings.

Two years before his death, Thutmose III made his son, Amenhotep II (1427–1393BC), his co-ruler. He was not called upon to emulate the military exploits of his father, but during the reign of his son, Thutmose IV (1393–1383BC), the power of the Hittites grew. To contain it, Thutmose IV made an alliance with his grandfather's old enemy, Mitanni, asking the Mitannian king, Artatama I, for his daughter's hand in marriage. Then, for nearly 40 years, there was peace in the western Asiatic empire, the warrior kings of the Eighteenth Dynasty having established Egypt as the dominant power, with diplomacy taking the place of warfare as the method of maintaining supremacy. New sources of wealth and an influx of immigrants from western Asia opened up Egypt as never before to foreign cultural influences in art, religion and language; and a great many Egyptians were enabled to indulge a taste for luxury and high living.

1. The rise of Amen-Re, King of the Gods

When Ahmose, founder of the Eighteenth Dynasty, reunited Egypt under his rule (*see* p.16), he chose his own native town to be the new capital of Egypt, retaining Inebhedj as the chief administrative centre. Very little is known of the early history of Ahmose's native town except that it had strategic importance due to its geographical position: it lay on both banks of the Nile, within easy reach of the natural resources of the Eastern and Western Deserts, whilst not far to the south lay Nubia, an invaluable source of manpower and gold. In spite of this, it was the nearby city of Iuny (modern Armant) which had until Ahmose's time been the capital of the administrative district in which both were situated. The district was called Waset (Sceptre) and Ahmose named his new capital city Waset in honour of it.

At least as early as the Twelfth Dynasty (1963–1786 BC), the chief god of Waset was Amun (**colour plate 1**), originally a deity of the air whose name means 'Hidden-' or 'Invisible-one'. In his honour, four kings of the Dynasty were named Amenemhat (Amun is the Foremost One); and four kings of the Eighteenth Dynasty were named Amenhotep (Amun is Pleased). In the Eighteenth Dynasty he became a god of war, and state god of Egypt. His priests proclaimed him to be a cosmic creator-god, self-engendered, who 'had no mother or father but shaped his own egg'. It was claimed that Waset was the birthplace of the whole universe, where the never-sleeping Amun ruled as 'Lord of Time who makes the years, rules the months, ordains nights and days'. Eventually, the priests added the name of the ancient sun god, Re, to that of Amun, and he became known as Amen-Re, King of the Gods (Amen Re Nesu Neteru), which the Greeks rendered as Amonrasonther.

Eventually, Waset became known as 'The City of Amun' or just as 'The City' — named in the Bible as No Amon (Nahum iii 8) and No (Ezekiel xxx 16). The Greeks equated Amun with Zeus and therefore called Waset 'Diospolis' (City of God). Homer named it Thebes, possibly as a compliment to the city in the Greek province of Boeotia whose most famous king was Oedipus, and described it as

> Proud Thebes ...
> The world's great empress on the Egyptian plain
> That spreads her conquests o'er a thousand states,
> And pours her heroes through a hundred gates,
> Two hundred horsemen and two hundred cars
> From each wide portal issuing to the wars.[9]

Today, the City of Amun lies in and under the modern town of Luxor, by which name the general public know it.

Amun's temple at Waset (**colour plate 2**), which was called *Ipt-swt*, meaning 'The Most Select of Places', was enlarged and embellished over the centuries, up to and including the Roman period. The site does not contain one temple only: it is, instead, a vast complex of religious buildings in which at least twenty major shrines have been identified. The sacred enclosure covers about half a square mile (1.25 sq.km) and the main temple, dedicated to Amun, was in its final phase nearly a mile (1.5 km) long. From the fourth century AD the temple, abandoned by its priests, was inhabited by local villagers and their animals. Gradually, it was buried under their debris until eventually only the tops of the windows in the main hall were visible, earning for it the Arabic name, Karnak — 'the town of the windows' — the name by which the site is known today.

Under Thutmose III, Waset became the capital of the empire that he won for Egypt in western Asia. Amun was given sovereignty over the deities of the countries that were subjugated, thus becoming the supreme god of the then-known world; and Thutmose III donated much of the wealth gained from his conquests in western Asia and Nubia to the city's chief deity, Amun. Thutmose III had good reason for such magnanimity. As he recorded in an inscription in the Temple of Amun at Waset, when he was a child, one of the minor sons of the King, he was serving as an acolyte in the Temple when his father came to make offerings to the God. Prince Thutmose was standing in the hall outside the Sanctuary as his father's procession passed by: and the God (presumably the statue of Amun, carried by priests in a portable shrine with carrying poles) began to search for him:

> On recognizing me, lo, he halted ... I threw myself on the pavement, I prostrated myself in his presence. He set me before him and I was placed at the Station of the King (i.e. the place usually occupied by the Ruler).[10]

And so, by means of a divine oracle, the young boy was chosen to be Crown Prince. The oracle, of course, must have been worked by the priests of Amun, who had marked out the young Thutmose and were prepared to back his claim to the throne.

Thutmose III's successors, Amenhotep II (1427–1393BC) and Thutmose IV (1392–1383BC), attributed their successes at home and abroad to the favour of Amun; and even claimed their rights to the throne of Egypt by virtue of the fact that each of them was the son of the god he spoke of as his 'father, Amun'. Throughout Egypt, new shrines and temples were built for Amun, often replacing those of other deities. Small chapels dedicated to these deities were erected within the precincts of Amun's own vast temple at Waset, thus emphasizing their subordination to him. The titles of High Priest of Re and High Priest of Ptah were included amongst the titles of the High Priest of Amun, who claimed superiority over all other priesthoods. He governed both the east bank at Waset, where the temples were situated, and the west bank where the great necropolis (*see* Glossary) of the city lay, and had charge not only of the royal tombs, and their memorial temples (*see* Glossary), but also of those of the nobles. Thus the dead as well as the living came under the jurisdiction of Amun's powerful priesthood.

2. Amenhotep III, Egypt's Sun King

Egypt was at the peak of political power and cultural development when Nebmaatre (Lord of Truth is Re) Amenhotep III (1383–1345BC) became King. The mummified body of his father, Thutmose IV, like many others, was removed from its own tomb in antiquity by priests anxious to preserve it against the depredations of tomb-robbers, and secreted in a side chamber of Amenhotep II's tomb in the royal necropolis at Waset,[11] where it was discovered in AD 1898. It is that of a balding, extremely emaciated man of about 30 years of age. The emaciation is thought not to have been the result of the mummification process but due to a wasting disease that contributed to the King's early demise. No child of Thutmose IV could have been much more than 15 years old at the time of the King's death and Amenhotep III must therefore have been a minor when he came to the throne.

Thutmose IV had married, for ceremonial reasons, his own mother, Tiaa,[12] and for diplomatic reasons a princess of Mitanni, but his two principal queens were his sister, Iaret, and Nefertari, who both bore the title Queen-in-Chief (*ḥmt nsw wrt* : literally, great royal wife). Amenhotep III's mother, however, was Mutemwiya (**1**), whose origins are uncertain but who appears to have been a commoner, a member of a family from Middle Egypt that was part of the powerful military class which had arisen with the creation of a standing army at the beginning of the Eighteenth Dynasty. Mutemwiya never bore the title Queen-in-Chief, and her known monumental inscriptions, which all date to the reign of her son, refer to her as 'Mother of the King' (*mwt nsw*), for whom she seems to have acted as regent until he reached his majority at the age of 15. Statues of the young Amenhotep III (**2**) depict him with a plump face, arched eyebrows, thick, sensual lips, and long, almond-shaped eyes; and a nose that is delicate with a rounded tip, unlike the prominent beaked noses of his royal forebears — a physiognomy that perhaps reflects his maternal rather than paternal ancestry.

During the first 11 years of the new reign, five important events were announced in novel fashion by means of inscriptions on the flat undersides of large commemorative stone scarabs, which were dispatched to all quarters of the Egyptian Empire. Examples have been discovered from as far afield as Ras Shamra in Syria to Soleb in Nubia. One set of 'news bulletin' scarabs, of which four still survive, is dated to the second year of Amenhotep III's reign, and records in detail that word was brought to the King, who was presumably in residence at Waset, that wild cattle had been sighted in the neighbourhood of what is today called Wadi Qena, near Koptos. He sailed downstream overnight, arriving at Wadi Qena in the early morning, when he ordered his military escort to trap the animals behind a rampart and ditch and count them: they numbered 170. Fifty-six of the wild cattle were then 'brought to' the King, presumably for him to shoot with his arrows as he

1.   *Queen Mutemwiya: statue head, limestone (Cairo Museum)*

*2. Amenhotep III:
statue head,
quartzite
(British
Museum)*

rode past in his chariot, but perhaps to lasso — the inscriptions on the scarabs do not explicitly state what happened, or even that any of the animals were actually killed. Amenhotep III then ordered a four-day rest for the horses before resuming the hunt, if that is what it can be termed. The total number of wild cattle caught was 96.

A second set of 'hunting scarabs' (**3**), of which 108 examples survive, was issued in the tenth year of Amenhotep III's reign to record the number of 'fierce' lions killed by the King in the first ten years of his reign — one hundred and two. Although it is stated on these scarabs that Amenhotep III killed these lions personally, it is possible that the scarabs were issued to prove that an otherwise indolent king was following in the sporting tradition that had been followed by his three immediate ancestors. Amenhotep III certainly did not emulate their military achievements, partly because, at the beginning of his reign, he did not have to. His military career seems to have consisted of an expedition to Nubia in the fifth year of his reign, although the rows of bound figures representing

3. *Lion hunt scarab of Amenhotep III [from J.Baikie, The Amarna Age, London, 1926, Pl. V]*

conquered foreign countries carved on the bases of temple walls and statue plinths were designed to suggest otherwise. It is ironic that Amenhotep III's Golden Horus Name (*see* Glossary) was 'Great of Strength who Smites the Asiatics' since it was his neglect of Egypt's possessions in western Asia that was to lead to the break-up of the Empire.

Another set of 'news bulletin' scarabs (**4**), of which 51 survive, was issued in the name of Amenhotep III coupled with that of his wife, Tiye. The inscription begins with the five names and epithets that made up the royal titulary and continues as follows: 'His Queen-in-Chief, Tiye, long may she live. The name of her father is Yuya and the name of her mother is Thuya. She is the wife of a mighty king whose southern border is at Karoy (near Napata in the Sudan), whose northern border is at Naharin (Mitanni).' These scarabs, which are undated, are often said to have been issued to proclaim the marriage of Amenhotep III and Tiye; but it is possible that they were issued to mark the King's accession by announcing the names that had been chosen for his titulary. If this is so, then

4. *Marriage scarab of Amenhotep III [Baikie, op. cit., Pl. V]*

it would seem that Amenhotep had been married to Tiye before he came to the throne. The wild cattle scarabs described above were issued in the names of both Tiye and Amenhotep III, so at the latest the pair were married by the second year of the reign, the date which appears on the scarabs.

On the scarabs Tiye's parents are referred to by their names only, without titles. This does not mean that Tiye was plucked from obscurity to marry the future King of Egypt; and considering that Tiye must have been a child no more than ten years old at the time, the marriage could scarcely have been a love match, although, by ancient Egyptian standards, she was nearing the age of puberty. It is probable that Prince Amenhotep had not been expected to inherit the throne and only did so because he survived brothers born of the Queens-in-Chief. Thus a marriage arranged between him and a daughter of a loyal military family, as Tiye apparently was, would have been acceptable. It has been suggested that Yuya was the brother of Queen Mutemwiya. If this were the case, then Mutemwiya, like many traditional Egyptian women of today, may have considered the ideal wife for her son to be her niece, especially if it were not envisioned that she would ever become Queen-in-Chief.

Tiye did, however, become Queen-in-Chief; and throughout her husband's long reign her position in his affections and as his confidant in matters of state was never threatened, despite Amenhotep contracting marriages with a series of foreign princesses — in the early part of his reign with Gilukhipa, daughter of King Shuttarna of Mitanni, and with a sister of Kadashman-Enlil, King of Babylon; and in the later part with Gilukhipa's niece, Tadukhipa, sister of King Tushratta of Mitanni, and with the daughters of Kadashman-Enlil and King Tarkhundaradu of Arzawa, in southern Anatolia. The marriage between Amenhotep III and Gilukhipa, which took place in the tenth year of his reign, was considered worthy of an issue of a set of commemorative scarabs, of which four have survived, to announce the: 'Marvels brought to His Majesty: Gilukhipa, daughter of Shuttarna, Prince of Naharin, together with most of her retinue consisting of 317 ladies-in-waiting'. All the ladies disappeared into the royal ménage, even Gilukhipa, of whom nothing is heard for 26 years until the negotiations for her niece's marriage took place, after which the luckless Gilukhipa seems to have died.[13] These scarabs were, of course, issued in the name of Amenhotep III: but Tiye's name appears in the place of honour after the King's. Her parentage is still stated baldly as 'her father's name is Yuya and her mother's name is Thuya' although by this time in Amenhotep III's reign he had conferred titles upon both Yuya and Thuya. The simple explanation for the lack of titles for them on the scarabs is that it was due to shortage of space or force of habit: but it could also be seen as a glorifying of the fact that Tiye was of humble origins.

A year after the marriage between Amenhotep III and Gilukhipa, another set of scarab 'news bulletins' was issued. On each scarab, the first day of the third month (September) of the Inundation Season is recorded as the day on which the preparation of a great irrigation basin, 3700 cubits (approximately 1700 metres) long by 700 cubits (approximately 325 metres) wide,[14] was begun on behalf of Tiye in her home town, Djarukha, near Ipu (*see* p. 39). The inscription goes on to record that 15 days later, the dykes that had been closed in order to hold back water in the catchment area were ceremonially opened by the King, who was rowed into the basin in the state barge, *Tekhen-Aten* (Radiance of the Aten), named after the hitherto minor sun god who was to rise to such importance. Once the water had seeped out, leaving a vast area of rich silt behind, the peasants would have planted seed in the fertile soil of Tiye's basin; and when the crops were eventually harvested, paid tax on them. Thus the purpose of the King's generous gift to Tiye was to provide the Queen with the revenues levied on an area of nearly 135 acres (55 hectares).

Through the strength of her personality, Tiye exercised an important influence on the reign not only of her husband, whom she outlived, but also on that of his successor, her son, Amenhotep IV, better known to posterity as Akhenaten. The words of King Tushratta of Mitanni in two letters that he sent to Amenhotep IV on his accession to the Egyptian throne are ample proof of Tushratta's recognition, at least, of Tiye's influence: 'As to all the words of Nimmuareya (the Babylonian/Akkadian version of Nebmaatre, the throne name of Amenhotep III), your father, which he wrote to me — Tiye, the beloved Queen-in-

5.   *Queen Tiye: yew wood head from Medinet el-Gurob, Faiyum (Ägyptisches Museum, Berlin)*

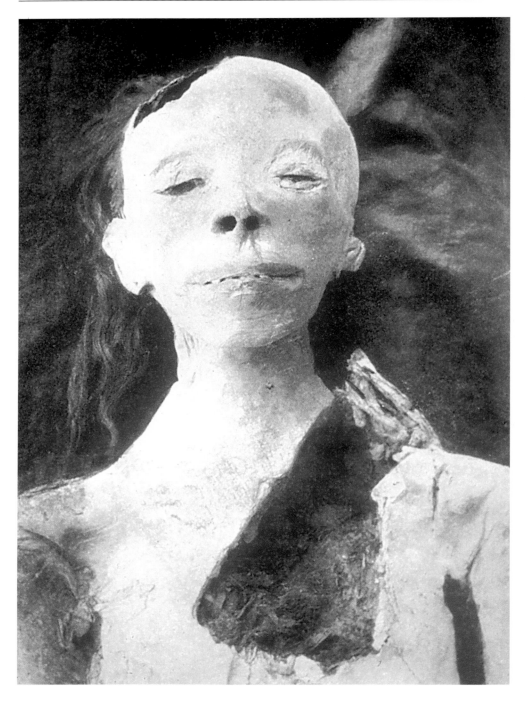

6.   *Prince Thutmose (?): mummy of young boy found in a side chamber of the tomb of
        Amenhotep II, Luxor [from G.E. Smith, Egyptian Mummies, in JEA, Vol. I, Part III, July
        1914, Plate XXXII, Fig.1.]*

Chief of Nimmuareya, your mother, she knows all about them. Ask Tiye, your mother, about all the words your father spoke to me.' 'Every single word that I discussed with your father, Tiye, your mother, knows them all; and no one else knows them.'[15]

Heretofore, a queen's highest status had not been as wife of the King, or daughter of the previous ruler, but as bearer of the title 'Mother of the King' (*mwt nsw*). Tiye was the first woman to exploit the position of Queen-in-Chief (*ḥmt nsw wrt*). In royal monumental statues and in reliefs in temples and private tombs she was prominently displayed at Amenhotep III's side in an unprecedented manner, never in a subservient fashion but playing a complementary role. Tiye was not only portrayed in the company of her husband but as an individual in her own right (**5**). Thus she was represented more often than any other ancient Egyptian queen with the exception of her daughter-in-law, Nefertiti. Her career reached its apogee in a cult-temple dedicated to her at Sedeinga in Upper Nubia, 54 miles (90 km) north of the Third Cataract of the Nile, where she was deified in her lifetime and worshipped alongside her husband as the patron deities of the region.

It is known that Tiye bore Amenhotep III at least two sons and five daughters. The elder son, Thutmose, died young; and if the body of a boy (**6**) discovered in AD1898 in a side chamber of Amenhotep II's tomb is indeed his, as some have claimed, then he was probably not much more than 11 years old when he died.[16] The second son, Amenhotep, succeeded his father on the throne (*see* p.26). Sitamun, whose name means 'Daughter of Amun', was the King's eldest daughter. When she was still a child she was accorded special status in inscriptions as the King's Chief Daughter; and by the 30th year of Amenhotep III's reign she had become her father's wife, with the title Queen-in-Chief, although there is no suggestion that Sitamun displaced her mother as Queen-in-Chief. Sitamun was given her own household; and a jar label found in the palace at Malkata (see p.31) shows that she was still alive in the 37th year of her father's reign, and may have outlived him. Her mummy may be that of the younger of the two women found in the same side chamber of the tomb of Amenhotep II (**7**) as the boy identified as Prince Thutmose. The other female mummy in the side chamber has been identified as that of Tiye (see p. 54).

The second daughter of Amenhotep III and Tiye was Henuttaneb, whose name was the same as a title borne by ancient Egyptian queens: 'Mistress of Every Land'. Although she is not known to have been a Queen-in-Chief, her status seems to have been similar to that of Tiye and Sitamun. In several monumental inscriptions her name is written within a *cartouche* (*see* Glossary); and in the colossal statue-group that is now in the Atrium of Cairo Museum (*see* p.32) she stands between her parents, although sculpted on a smaller scale, wearing a crown and wig identical to those worn by her mother. Henuttaneb therefore may very well have been one of her father's wives. A third daughter, Aset (in Greek, Isis), who was named after the wife of Osiris, the most popular God of the Underworld, certainly was, and in inscriptions she is referred to as Royal Wife (*ḥmt nsw*) with her name written inside a *cartouche*. The fourth daughter of Amenhotep III and Tiye, Nebetah (Lady of the Palace), appears in the statue-group referred to above, but is otherwise unknown. The fifth daughter, Beketaten (Servant of the Aten), seems to have been a child of the royal couple's old age and is known only from monuments dating to her brother's reign.

Amenhotep III is dubbed 'the Magnificent' because of the size and ambition of his architectural undertakings and for the number of representations of himself that he

7. *Side-chamber, tomb of Amenhotep II [Postcard, c.1945]*

commissioned. Well over a thousand representations of the King, in the form of sculptured reliefs, tomb-paintings and statues ranging in size from the small-scale to the colossal, have survived, an indication that he had himself depicted more frequently than any other ancient Egyptian king. Such a high volume of artistic output bears testimony to the generosity of royal patronage; and to the favourable economic circumstances of the reign. In contrast to the reigns of Thutmose III and his immediate successors, when much of Egypt's wealth was made up of the spoils of conquest, wealth in Amenhotep III's time accrued from international trade and the ability to recover abundant supplies of gold either from mining in the Eastern Desert or by panning gold dust in Nubia.

At Waset, Amenhotep III ordered a great pylon-gateway, the Third Pylon, to be built on the west side of the Temple of Amun, a project that involved the clearance of several earlier structures, including a colonnaded forecourt built for his own father, Thutmose IV. The interior of the new pylon-gateway was packed with hundreds of sculptured blocks from the dismantled buildings, notably those from a beautifully decorated limestone kiosk (**colour plate 3**) built for the Twelfth-Dynasty King, Senwosret I (1943–1898BC), that was retrieved and reassembled in modern times and is now the chief exhibit in the Open-air Museum at Karnak. Amenhotep III's first major building project was the magnificent edifice that stands relatively intact today, and which is now known as Luxor Temple (**colour plate 4**). It was erected a short distance to the south of the Temple of Amun and its chief glories are an imposing double colonnade of fourteen columns and, beyond it, a vast open courtyard surrounded on three sides by double rows of columns, as elegant as any ever built in Egypt. The temple, which was called *Ipt-rsy* (the Private Apartments of

8.   *Colossi of Memnon, Luxor. David Roberts lithograph, 1838.*

the South), was dedicated to Amun; but it was also the edifice in which Amenhotep III's 'divine birth' was celebrated. On the walls of a side chamber reliefs inspired by a similar set from the memorial temple of the Female King, Hatshepsut, at Deir el-Bahari, recorded that Amun, in the guise of Thutmose IV, impregnated Queen Mutemwiya with the son who became Amenhotep III.

Amenhotep III had several palaces throughout Egypt but his principal royal residence, called 'Radiance of the Aten', a favourite epithet (*see* p.26), was a vast complex of buildings on the west bank of the Nile at Waset, known today by the Arabic name for the site, Malkata, or 'The Place of Picking Things Up'. With separate palaces for the King, Tiye, Sitamun and possibly the Crown Prince, not to mention living quarters for princesses, foreign dignitaries and court nobility, audience chambers, a temple dedicated to Amun, administrative buildings, servants' quarters, kitchens, granaries, stables, cattle byres and workshops, the labyrinthine complex was a veritable town covering about 80 acres (32 hectares). There was even a great man-made harbour, now dry and known as Birket Habu. It gave direct access to the Nile a short distance to the east; and its size, some one and five-eighths of a mile (2.6km) long by five-eighths of a mile (1km) wide, gives an indication of the amount of traffic arriving at the royal residence. The structures within the palace complex were single-storey buildings largely made of mud brick, as was the norm, with some stone and wood. The palaces, however, were decorated with faience tiles in a variety of colours, their interior walls covered with plaster painted with exquisite murals. It cannot be doubted that the quality of their furnishings reflected refined taste and fine workmanship.

A huge, rock-cut tomb, now numbered W(est)V(alley) 22, was prepared for Amenhotep III in the western branch of the Valley of the Tombs of the Kings at Waset.[17] Its associated memorial temple, erected at what is now called Kom el-Hetan on the plain to the east of the Valley, seems to have been the largest of its type ever constructed. Named 'The Mansion of Amun on the West of Waset', it was, according to a stele (*see* Glossary) discovered at the temple site, 'wrought with gold throughout, its floors adorned with silver and all its doors with fine gold.'[18] Sadly, it was almost completely dismantled by later kings: but the two colossal statues (**8**) of Amenhotep III seated on a throne that once stood before the temple's pylon-gateway remain, dominating the cultivated fields that surround them. Each colossus was carved from a single sandstone block and, even without the plinth, is nearly 18m high. Today the statues are known as the Colossi of Memnon, although in the Graeco-Roman period only the northern colossus (**colour plate 5**) was identified with Memnon.

The northern colossus was damaged by an earthquake that struck the Theban area in 27BC. In his *Geography*, Strabo (64BC– *c*.AD25) records that he visited the colossi with the Roman Governor of Egypt, Aelius Gallus, and heard the noise 'as of a slight blow' that was said to emanate from the northern monument once each day, although he was suspicious that the sound had been produced by one of the men who clustered round it.[19] Other Greek travellers were not so sceptical and came to hear the phenomenon. They had probably never heard of Amenhotep III and claimed that the statue was that of Memnon, son of the dawn goddess, Eo. During the Trojan War, he killed Antilochus, son of Nestor, and was then himself killed by Achilles. After his death, Memnon took the form of the colossus at West Waset and, each dawn, could be heard crying for his mother. A number of inscriptions on the legs and feet of the colossus record, sometimes not inelegantly, the visits of important persons who had 'heard the Memnon'. Amongst these was the Emperor Hadrian, who, in AD130, camped for several days before Memnon, wisely accompanied by an accomplished poetess, Julia Balbilla, whose verses, carved upon one of the feet, relate that, in the presence of the Ruler of the World, Memnon said 'Good morning' without waiting for the sun. The Emperor Septimus Severus (AD193–211) had the colossus repaired; and it has remained silent ever since.

Large-scale statues of Amenhotep III (**9 & 10**) were most often placed inside temples, not least in Ipt-rsy at Waset (*see* p.30), where many were later usurped by Ramesses II (1279–1213BC). The favourite medium was red or black granite; but white limestone was used for the colossal statue-group (**11**) that now stands in the Atrium of Cairo Museum. The statue-group depicts Amenhotep III seated on a throne with Tiye beside him. Their daughter, Henuttaneb, stands between them; by the side of Amenhotep III's right leg is their daughter, Nebetah; and by the side of Tiye's left leg is another daughter, Aset. The princesses, depicted on the whole as miniature versions of their mother, are sculpted on a smaller scale than their parents, but as this was a convention of Egyptian art, no matter the age of the child when depicted with its parents, there is no way of telling how old the princesses were when the statue was made. The expressions on the faces of the King and Queen are youthful and serene, their mouths, with dimples at the corners, smiling: the faces are, in fact, remarkably alike.

The statue-group, which may originally have been erected in the palace at Malkata,

9. *Amenhotep III:
statue head, black
granite (British
Museum)*

was discovered in AD1892 in the nearby Memorial Temple of Ramesses III at Medinet
Habu. It was smashed into pieces but with the figures of the King and Queen almost
intact; and was restored by Alexandre Barsanti (*see* p.140). It is over 7m high, but does
not compare in size to the Colossi of Memnon. Even they, however, would have been
dwarfed by the statue that once stood before the Tenth Pylon-gateway in the Temple of
Amun at Waset. All that have survived of this colossus are the feet, placed one in advance
of the other suggesting that the statue was that of a standing figure. Using the feet —
which are 2.90m long — as a basis for calculation, it has been estimated that the statue
was at least 21m high.

10.   *Amenhotep III: statue, black granite (British Museum)*

11.   *Amenhotep III and Tiye with, from left to right, princesses Nebetah, Henuttaneb and Aset,
limestone statue from Medinet Habu,Luxor (Cairo Museum)*

In the last decade of his reign, Amenhotep III celebrated three jubilees or *heb-sed* festivals, in Regnal Years 30, 34 and 37. The *heb-sed* was a very ancient ritual designed to re-invigorate a king by ritual means, ideally after 30 years on the throne, but 'topped up' by further *heb-seds* if the king lived long enough. Amenhotep III celebrated his *heb-seds* at Malkata in a hall, 'The Mansion of Rejoicing' (*Per Hai*), that was specially constructed for the purpose. Jar labels found at the site indicate that vast quantities of food and drink were provided for the occasion, which was celebrated with feasting, singing and dancing, and the presentation of fine gifts to the guests. Amenhotep III seems to have interpreted his first *heb-sed* not merely as a re-invigoration but as a means by which he was restored symbolically to youth. Statues dating to the period after the first *heb-sed* are unique in that they portray a king who in actuality was well over 40 years old as having the face of a young boy, with wide-open eyes, turned-up nose and a mouth in which the upper lip is fuller than the lower, like that of baby who has just been fed.[20] In contrast, a contemporary head of Tiye (**12**), made of steatite and found at Serâbit el-Khâdim in Sinai, shows her with lined features and a mouth down-turned at the corners, a more realistic representation of a mature woman in all her imperious dignity.

Amenhotep III seems to have taken the celebration of his *heb-seds* as an opportunity to emphasise his divinity. A King of Egypt had always been regarded as the earthly manifestation of the god, Horus, with the epithet 'the good god' frequently attached to his name. Amenhotep III went a step further: he deified himself; and in the large cult-temple at Soleb, near Sedeinga in Upper Nubia, built at the time of his first *heb-sed*, he was worshipped jointly with Amun, not under his birth name, Amenhotep, but under his Throne Name, Nebmaatre. In reliefs in the temple he was depicted making offerings to his alter ego, deified in the guise of a lunar god: thus the King, Nebmaatre Amenhotep, with his birth and throne names written in *cartouches*, can be seen worshipping the God, Nebmaatre, whose name is not written inside a *cartouche*.

Towards the end of his reign, Amenhotep III laid stress on his divine self-regeneration. This is made clear by two diorite statues of the King that were found in the ruins of his Memorial Temple and date to the period of his last *heb-sed*. Originally slightly larger than life-sized, the statues are damaged and have lost their heads and legs: but it is the torsos of these statues that make them unique. The bottom part of a square-cut beard of the type that was peculiar to Ptah, the creator-god of Inebhedj, is still visible. The breasts are pendulous and the hands are clasped together over a swollen belly. The King wears a V-necked cloak with braided edges; and the carving indicates that the cloak is transparent. When looked at sideways on, the breasts and bellies of the statues are reminiscent of those of the hippopotamus-goddess, Taweret, who personified fecundity. Thus the statues clearly identified Amenhotep III with creation and fertility, and presumably were meant to suggest that he was a living god who recreated himself eternally.

A notable feature of the Eighteenth Dynasty was the opportunity given to a man of talent not related to the royal family to rise to a position of power. Throughout his reign, Amenhotep III was fortunate in having the services of several extremely talented men at his disposal. The most important amongst these administrators were Ramose, Chief Minister of Upper Egypt, and Amenhotep, Chief Minister of Lower Egypt; Merymose, Viceroy of Kush, responsible for keeping control over Nubia, Egypt's main source of gold;

12.   *Queen Tiye: steatite head from Serâbit el-Khâdim, Sinai (Cairo Museum)*

13. Tomb of Ramose, Luxor: finely sculpted heads in raised relief

Merya and Ptahmose, Chancellors; Meryptah, the Chief Treasurer; and Khaemhet, Royal Scribe and Overseer of the Granaries of Upper and Lower Egypt. There was also Surere, the Chief Steward; and Kheruef, Steward of Queen Tiye's estates. Over 20 of these officials had tombs in the Theban necropolis, with those of Ramose (**colour plate 6**), Khaemhet, Kheruef and Surere[21] having walls carved in superb raised relief (**13**) depicting scenes of daily life that illustrate the refined taste and high standards of gracious living (**14**) that marked Amenhotep III's reign.

The outstanding figure of the reign, a man who for later generations of Egyptians eclipsed even the King himself, proved to be Amenhotep-son-of-Hapu, who came from an obscure family from Kem-wer (modern Tell Atrib (Greek Athribis) in the Delta, but who rose to become overseer of all the King's works, royal scribe, scribe of recruits and steward of the estates of the princess, Sitamun. He never held the important post of Chief Minister, although one who did, Ramose (*see* p.36), was a relative. It was the King's namesake who engineered the building of Ipt-rsy Temple and of the colossi in the Temple of Amun and at Amenhotep III's Memorial Temple (*see* p.36); but we can only speculate about the reasons why this humble but loyal servant of the King was honoured with a memorial temple on the west bank at Waset that was comparable to the royal temples nearby, and with a statue of himself erected within the hallowed precincts of the Temple of Amun. Amenhotep-son-of-Hapu, who lived to the age of eighty, was revered by later generations as a sage; and in the Graeco-Roman period he was worshipped as a god of healing, with a sanctuary at Deir el-Bahri.

Although Amenhotep III never appointed his father-in-law to any of the great offices of state such as Chief Minister or Treasurer, by the end of his life Yuya had had some 40 titles

14. *Statuette of servant girl (Oriental Museum, University of Durham)*

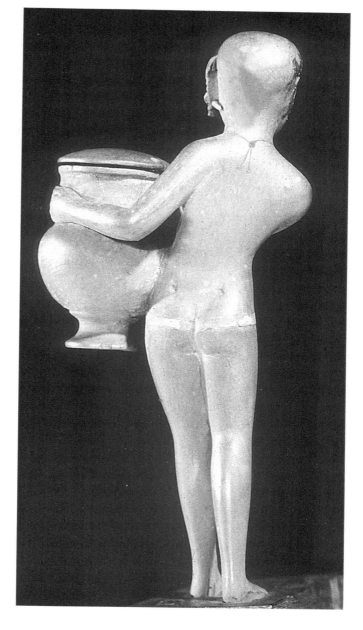

conferred upon him, including Prince, Royal Confidant, First Among the King's Companions, Lieutenant-General of the King's Chariots, Lord of Ipu, High Priest of Min and Father of the God. Father of the God was usually a priestly office, but it is probable that in this instance it meant father-in-law of the King. Ipu (modern-day Akhmim), which lay on the east bank of the Nile some 96 miles (160 km) north of Waset, was the capital of the Ninth District of Upper Egypt and a centre for the worship of the fertility-god, Min. The fact that two of his titles — Lord of Ipu, and High Priest of Min — connect Yuya to Ipu may indicate that this was his place of origin.

15. *Yuya: mummy mask (Cairo Museum)*

16.   *Thuya: head of mummy (Cairo Museum)*

Thuya bore several titles, including one which connected her also with Min, that of Mistress of the Womens' Apartments in the Temple of Min. She was also a Royal Ornament, an epithet describing a lady of the royal court, Mistress of the Robes, Chantress of Amun and Superintendent of the Womens' Apartments in the Temple of Amun. Thuya's most important title, however, was Mother of the Great Royal Wife. She was also, according to inscriptions on her sarcophagus (*see* Glossary) and coffin, the mother of a son, Aanen, who served Amun as a second-rank 'Servant-of-the-God-Priest'. Titles in ancient Egypt were a mixture of job descriptions and honorary positions; and the more titles a person held, the greater his or her status in society. Between them, Yuya and Thuya held an appreciable number but the highest honour paid to them was the gift of a tomb, now numbered KV46[22] in the Valley of the Tombs of the Kings, an honour bestowed on only a very few who were not royal.

The tomb is quite small, has only one chamber and is undecorated; but when it was discovered almost intact on 5 February 1905 by the English archaeologist, James E. Quibell (1867–1935), working for his sponsor, Theodore M. Davis (see p.107), the quantity and quality of its funerary furnishings amazed the excavators. The mummified body of Yuya, his head covered by a gilded mask (**15**),[23] was housed in three nested wooden mummy-cases set within a huge rectangular wooden sarcophagus; and his preserved viscera were placed inside four calcite canopic jars with portrait lids which were in turn placed inside a lidded wooden box set on a sledge. Thuya's body was housed in a similar manner, except that she had only two mummy-cases. The bodies of Yuya and Thuya are considered to be two of the finest specimens produced by the practitioners of

17. *Chair of Sitamun (Cairo Museum)*

mummification. The couple probably died within a few years of each other in the third decade of Amenhotep III's reign, he a handsome, white-haired man in his early sixties, with a prominent, beaked nose (**colour plate 8**), she an old lady approaching sixty, of typical Egyptian appearance (**16**) and less than five feet tall.

Apart from an extensive range of ritual items, the tomb contents included Yuya's chariot, several pairs of leather and woven papyrus sandals that had been worn in life, and a rushwork chest containing Thuya's wig. There were also three beds; two chests, gifts from Yuya and Thuya's royal son-in-law; and three splendid chairs, gifts from their grand-daughter, Queen-Princess Sitamun. The tops of the front legs of one of the chairs are decorated with rare portrait-heads of Sitamun (**17**); and when Quibell first opened the tomb another chair, its arms carved with ibexes, still had on its seat a linen cushion filled with down.

It would seem that in the last few years of his reign Amenhotep III was ailing: on a painted sandstone stele (*see* p. 53) found at Tell el-Amarna he is depicted as decidedly corpulent and unhealthy-looking; and if the mummified body discovered in his grandfather's tomb is indeed his,[24] he was suffering from painful alveolar abscesses on his gums. However, the fact that he was not at the peak of physical fitness did not deter Amenhotep III from adding to his collection of western Asiatic princesses; and in the 36th

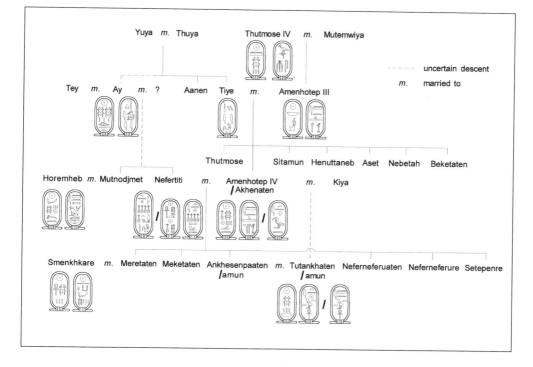

Fig. 2. The Royal family at the end of the Eighteenth Dynasty

year of his reign he sent to the new King of Mitanni, Tushratta, requesting the hand of his sister, Tadukhipa, in marriage. In the same year, Amenhotep III made another request: that Tushratta send him the statue of the Babylonian goddess of love and war, Ishtar, from her temple in Nineveh, in the hope that the statue's famed healing powers would help him. Tushratta sent the statue — but he was to find difficulty in persuading Amenhotep III to return it, not surprisingly since the statue was proving to be so effective that Amenhotep III was able to celebrate his third *heb-sed* in Year 37! Indeed, a number of jar labels from Malkata bear the date, Year 38, making it clear that Amenhotep III lived for at least two years after his request for Ishtar's statue, and possibly slightly longer: the exact date of his death is unknown. As for Tadukhipa: on the death of Nebmaatre Amenhotep III she, like Egypt, was inherited by his son and successor, Neferkheperure (Beautiful are the Manifestations of Re) Amenhotep IV.

3 Akhenaten and Nefertiti

Neferkheperure Amenhotep IV (1353–1337BC) was destined to become in modern times the most discussed monarch ever to rule Egypt. He has been the subject of countless academic studies, the hero of many novels, and, sung by a countertenor, the protagonist in an opera.[25] He has even inspired a play, *Akhnaten*, written, in a departure from her normal genre, detective fiction, by Agatha Christie in a style that is pastiche Noel Coward! No other king in the 3000-year-long history of ancient Egypt has aroused such passions, many of them contradictory, in those studying his reign. He has been admired as a visionary who made a valiant attempt to wean the ancient Egyptians away from their traditional polytheism in favour of an enlightened monotheism, in pursuit of which he instigated a revolutionary and much admired new style of art; and was condemned as a king who neglected to fulfil his traditional duties and brought Egypt to the brink of ruin. His 17-year-long reign, known today as the Amarna Age, is undoubtedly one of the most fascinating eras in Egyptian history.

In the nineteenth century, many leading Egyptologists were committed Christians who found Amenhotep IV-Akhenaten a sympathetic figure, their own monotheism leading them to admire his. He was identified as the first monotheist in history; and in his book, *Moses and Monotheism*, the psychiatrist, Sigmund Freud, claimed that Akhenaten was the inspiration for the religious beliefs of Moses. James Henry Breasted (1865–1935), the father of American Egyptology, saw Akhenaten as the first individual in history, 'the world's first idealist ... the earliest monotheist ... stepping out from the long line of conventional and colorless Pharaohs that he might disseminate ideas far beyond and above the capacity of his age to understand'.[26] Arthur Weigall (1880–1934), the English Egyptologist whose publications helped to popularize Akhenaten, was wildly inventive in his vision of the King, picturing him as 'a pale and sickly youth' with a head that was 'too large for his body', searching for 'that happiness which his physical condition had denied him.' He went on to imagine Akhenaten's eyes as 'wells of dream' and claimed that his delicately moulded features and mouth (**18**) were reminiscent of the best work of the Pre-Raphaelite painter, Dante Gabriel Rossetti. Weigall claimed that with Akhenaten it was possible to look into his mind and see something of its working; and that 'all that is there observed is worthy of admiration'.

Others have not been so complimentary. To some, Akhenaten was far from being a man in advance of his time, a forerunner of Christ. The doyen of twentieth-century Egyptologists, Sir Alan Gardiner (1879–1963), thought him a fanatic; the archaeologist, John Pendlebury (*see* p. 140) considered him a religious maniac; and, in the opinion of another Egyptologist, S.R.K. Glanville (1900–1956), Akhenaten as a king was deserving of

18.   *Akhenaten: model head in plaster from workshop of sculptor, Thutmose, Tell el-Amarna (Ägyptisches Museum, Berlin)*

nothing but censure. It has been claimed that he was the historical precedent for the Oedipus legend,[27] and that his supposed subservience to his mother made him the first man to be afflicted with what modern psychiatrists term an Oedipus complex. Nevertheless, the traditional view of the Amarna Age has been that it was the romantic and beautiful story of a king, Akhenaten, the child of a father, Amenhotep III, who was lazy and indolent, and a mother, Tiye, who was dominant and influential, instilling in her young son her own religious beliefs. It is also seen to be the story of the husband of a wife, Nefertiti, who was one of the most beautiful women the world has seen. He was proud to make public demonstrations of their love for each other, but their happiness was clouded by the fact that she could not give him a son, bearing one daughter after another in the attempt to do so.

In many respects, the Amarna Age is very well documented; and the main outlines of its history clear. In spite of this, the evidence that would lead to a solution of the many problems posed by the period is often lacking. Since the scientific study of ancient Egypt began in the nineteenth century, more has been written about Amarna than any other period of Egyptian history: but in the story of Amarna it is often difficult to disentangle myth from fact, speculation from reality. Interpretations of Akhenaten's character have changed over the years in the light of contemporary prejudices and preoccupations. He has gone from the Victorian view of him as an ideal father and husband, living a life of pacifism and religious devotion, to the late twentieth-century view of him as essentially a humanist who believed only in what he could see and rejected the mystical. In modern times he has become for some a debunked hero, for others a character who attracts fanatical devotion; and in the light of on-going research which might lead to further enlightenment, it can only be a matter of time before the character of this enigmatic king is re-asssessed yet again. To paraphrase a Bob Marley song: 'there are more questions than (definitive) answers' about the Amarna Age, and this is what makes it one of the most fascinating periods in Egyptian history.

The arguments about Akhenaten's reign begin at the beginning, for there is controversy over when exactly it started. The reigns of Amenhotep III and Amenhotep IV may have overlapped in what Egyptologists call a co-regency, although it might better be described as an associative kingship. Such an arrangement had been known before — in the Twelfth Dynasty, when Amenemhat I (1963–1934BC) shared the throne for nine years with his son, Senwosret I (1943–1898BC), Senwosret I shared it for three years with his son, Amenemhat II (1901–1866BC), and Amenemhat II shared the throne for two years with his son, Senwosret II (1901–1866BC); and in the Eighteenth Dynasty when, a couple of years before he died, Amenhotep III's great-grandfather, Thutmose III, associated his son, Amenhotep II, on the throne with him. The purpose of the arrangement was to allow an old, perhaps infirm, king to devolve some of his responsibilities upon his physically more active son, with the added, perhaps more important, advantage that it made clear the royal succession. Although some might think that Amenhotep IV hardly qualified as physically active, there seems to be enough evidence[28] to suggest that Amenhotep III associated his son on the throne with him for a decade or so, thus dating the reign of Neferkheperure Amenhotep IV (Akhenaten) to 1355–1337BC.

Amenhotep IV's chief wife was Nefertiti, whose name means 'The Beautiful Woman is

Present'. He seems to have married her before coming to the throne, as his father had married Tiye; but in contrast to Yuya and Thuya, the names of Nefertiti's parents are nowhere recorded. She is certainly never called 'King's Daughter'. It was once thought that she was the Mitannian princess, Tadukhipa, who had been sent to Egypt to marry Amenhotep III but had instead married his son and been given a new, Egyptian, name. However, the influential art historian and Egyptologist, Cyril Aldred (1914–1991), was convinced by H.W. Fairman, Brunner Professor of Egyptology at Liverpool Univerisity, 1948–1974, that Nefertiti was the daughter of Ay, who became King ten years after Amenhotep IV's death (*see* p. 129).[29] Aldred postulated the theory[30] that Ay was the son of Yuya and Thuya, even though only one son, Aanen, is connected with them on inscriptional evidence (*see* p. 41). He argued that Ay held many of the same offices and titles as Yuya; and that both men were connected with the Ipu region, where Ay held official positions and where Yuya's daughter, Tiye, owned extensive estates. Ay later built a rock-chapel there dedicated to the god, Min. On the basis of this circumstantial evidence, Aldred suggested that two men, near-contemporaries of each other, who both hailed from the same small provincial city and whose titles and careers were closely parallel, must surely be father and son, with Ay succeeding his father, Yuya, in 'the time-honoured Egyptian tradition'. In recent years it has become accepted that Ay was indeed the son of Yuya and Thuya and thus the brother-in-law of Amenhotep III.

The theory that Ay was Tiye's brother and Nefertiti's father is attractive because it would have allowed history to repeat itself: just as Queen Mutemwiya had witnessed her son marrying her niece, Tiye, so Queen Tiye would have witnessed her son marrying her niece, Nefertiti. The identity of Nefertiti's mother, however, is unknown. Ay was married to a woman called Tey, who bore the titles Royal Ornament and Leading Chantress of Waenre (The Unique One Who Belongs to Re i.e. Akhenaten), making her an important lady of the royal court. She also bore the titles Nurse of the Queen-in-Chief (Nefertiti), Governess of the Goddess, and One Who Praises the Queen-in-Chief. Because Tey is nowhere recorded as Nefertiti's mother but only her nurse and governess, it is assumed that she was her stepmother, in which case Nefertiti must have been Ay's daughter by a wife who died when Nefertiti was very young but about whom nothing is as yet known.

Nefertiti (**colour plate 9**) enjoyed the same relationship to Amenhotep IV as Tiye to Amenhotep III: she was his equal and in reliefs was shown at his side on state occasions, her name frequently inscribed alongside his, resplendent in the distinctive, tall, flat-topped, blue headdress[31] with which she was to be forever identified. The tombs of Akhenaten's courtiers were decorated with unprecedented scenes of the royal couple's intimate life together, often showing them demonstrating their affection not only for each other but for their children (**19**). From the earliest years of the reign, Nefertiti appeared in official art playing an unusually prominent role: in parts of the decoration of the temples built for the Aten at Waset (*see* p.51), for example, her figure eclipses that of the King. Such prominence is all the more surprising given her supposed origins. Even more surprising is the depiction of the Queen in a relief from Khemenu[32] in which she is shown in the traditional pose of a warrior king, in the act of smiting with her mace a captive enemy whom she holds pinioned by his hair (*see* p.52).

It is known that Nefertiti bore Akhenaten six daughters. The eldest, Meretaten

19. *Akhenaten and Nefertiti with, from left to right, princesses Meretaten, Meketaten and Ankhesenpaaten: shrine stele, limestone (Ägyptisches Museum, Berlin)*

(Beloved of the Aten), was probably born before the start of her father's reign since she was old enough to be depicted standing behind her mother as she officiated in the Aten Temple at Waset,[33] a little girl dressed as an adult woman, clasping a sistrum (*see* Glossary) in her hand. The second daughter, Meketaten (Protected by the Aten), must have been born in the early years of the reign; and she too was depicted in the Aten Temple at Waset.[34] The third daughter, Ankhesenpaaten (May She Live for the Aten), seems to have been born in the seventh year of Akhenaten's reign, at which time she begins to appear on royal monuments (*see* p. 72). The fourth daughter, named Neferneferuaten after her mother (*see* p. 51), with the epithet Tasherit (the Younger) appended, was born within a year or so of Ankhesenpaaten; and the fifth daughter, Neferneferure (Perfect is the Goodness of Re), in the ninth year of her father's reign (**colour plate 7**). The sixth and last daughter of Akhenaten and Nefertiti was Setepenre (Chosen by Re). Very little is known about her and she, like several of her sisters, seems to have died in childhood.

For many years Egyptologists thought that Amenhotep IV had been monogamous. His admirers accepted that Tadukhipa was apparently his wife, but maintained that it was a marriage in name only: nothing must be allowed to tarnish Akhenaten's image as the devoted husband of the beautiful Nefertiti. But then, in 1959, the American Egyptologist, William C. Hayes (1903–1963), in his guide to the Egyptian collections in the

Metropolitan Museum of Art in New York,[35] drew attention to the inscription on a small calcite cosmetic pot; and in the early 1960s, H.W. Fairman published a description of the pieces of a similar pot that had recently been acquired by the British Museum. Both pots contained the name Kiya in their inscriptions, which referred to 'the greatly beloved wife (*ḥmt mrrty ʿ3t*) of the King of Upper and Lower Egypt, who lives on Truth, Lord of the Two Lands, Neferkheperure-Waenre (Akhenaten), the beautiful child of the living Aten, who shall live for ever and ever: Kiya.'[36] In the ensuing years, more evidence relating to Kiya has come to light in the form of inscribed objects[37] and reliefs, mostly from excavations at El-Amarna, that show her performing religious rites alone, or accompanying the King at official ceremonies in the manner of Nefertiti, although, it must be noted, the two Queens never appear together. The origins of Kiya are unknown. It has been suggested that it is she rather than Nefertiti who is to be identified with the Mitannian princess, Tadukhipa, who was mentioned by that name several times in the contemporary diplomatic correspondence now known as the Amarna Letters (*see* p. 135), but only until the fourth year of Amenhotep IV's reign. It is possible that Tadukhipa's name then disappeared from the correspondence because she had died; but it is also possible that at that time she was for some reason given more prominence at Court, possibly because she had borne a son (*see* p.52). Her Mitannian name may have been abbreviated to its third and fourth syllables, 'khipa' and Egyptianized to 'Kiya', which, ironically, is derived from the word 'other' or 'another'. Nefertiti's opinion of 'the other woman' in her husband's life is not recorded.

In inscriptions dating to the later years of Akhenaten's reign, carved on blocks surviving from dismantled temples and palaces at Waset and Khemenu,[38] the names of two princesses appear: Meretaten-Tasherit (the Younger) and Ankhesenpaaten-Tasherit. It has been suggested that they were named after the eldest and third-eldest daughters of the King because they were the children of these princesses; and that it was very probably the King himself who had fathered them. However, if Ankhesenpaaten was born in the seventh year of her father's reign, she would have been too young to have been the mother of her namesake. It is more probable, therefore, that Kiya was the mother of Ankhesenpaaten-Tasherit; and although it is possible that she was the mother of Meretaten-Tasherit also, it is likely that the elder Meretaten bore this child of Akhenaten's.

In ancient Egypt, brother-sister marriages were not unknown, and were sanctified by the myth of Osiris and Isis, very popular deities who were both siblings and man and wife. Such marriages were especially common in the royal family, since property passed through the female line and a king was constrained to marry regardless of consanguinity in the interests of maintaining the royal line of inheritance. Marriage between father and daughter, when that father was the king, may have been more common than existing records show. Amenhotep IV was not the first king to marry his own daughters: his father had married several of his; and it is possible that in these marriages both kings were attempting to safeguard their godheads as manifestations of the Aten (*see* Chapter 4). Ramesses II in the following Dynasty was to follow their example in marrying several of his daughters. Thus, although some of Akhenaten's admirers might find his incestuous unions, especially if they produced children, unpalatable, severely damaging as they are to his image as the ideal Victorian paterfamilias, they were acceptable to the ancient Egyptians.

The coronation of Neferkheperure Amenhotep IV was performed in the Temple of Amun at Waset in the customary Eighteenth-Dynasty way. Amun was still the state god of Egypt, although Amenhotep III had long since become convinced of the necessity of curbing the power of his priesthood. At the beginning of his reign, the office of High Priest of Amun and that of Chief Minister of Upper Egypt were both held by one man, Ptahmose. By the end of the reign, the two posts had been separated, with the High Priest of Amun being restricted to religious duties and having no say in politics. As a further counter to Amun's priesthood, Amenhotep III acknowledged the cult of Ptah by appointing his son, Thutmose, High Priest of Ptah, a symbolic move since Thutmose must have been a child at the time. Amenhotep III also began to promote the worship of a sun god, the Aten, hitherto a minor aspect of Re-Horakhty, one of Egypt's most ancient solar deities.

Early in his reign, Amenhotep IV ordered a temple to the Aten to be built at Waset, immediately to the east of the Temple of Amun. Parts of the new temple, it is thought, were integrated into the old. Nevertheless, after Akhenaten's death, the Temple of the Aten was dismantled and the sandstone blocks from which it had been constructed were either dispersed for use in other building projects, or used as in-filler for two colossal gateways built for the Temple of Amun, the Second and Ninth Pylon-gateways. Between AD1946 and 1949, the French archaeologist, Henri Chevrier was in charge of the dismantling of the northern wing of the Second Pylon-gateway so that it might be repaired. He found thousands of decorated blocks inside it and recognized them immediately as the distinctive, small blocks that were nearly all of a uniform size, measuring roughly 53 x 23 x 25.5cm, which had been used at Waset exclusively for buildings of the Amarna period. Hundreds more of them had already been discovered during work on the Ninth Pylon-gateway. By the mid 1960s over 45,000 blocks, known to Egyptologists by the Arabic term *talatat*, had been retrieved; and in the 1970s the task of photographing them and attempting to reconstruct the temple using a computer was begun by a team of Egyptologists known as the Akhenaten Temple Project.

Even before the Temple of the Aten at Waset had been completed, Akhenaten determined to transfer his court away from the domain of Amun; and in the fourth year of his reign, perhaps earlier, he ordered work to begin on a new city where the worship of the Aten could flourish without interference. A site some 200 miles (330km) north of Waset was chosen for the city, which was to be called Akhetaten (Horizon of the Aten), today better known as Tell el-Amarna. If there was indeed an associative kingship between Amenhotep IV and his father, it may have been in their minds that two courts were necessary, with the senior king staying in Waset, the old religious capital, and the younger removing himself to Akhetaten, the better to promote the worship of the Aten, whose cause he had taken up with great zeal. By the fifth year of his reign, the new King had changed his name from Amenhotep (Amun is Satisfied) to Akhenaten (Glorified Spirit of the Aten); and Nefertiti's name had been prefixed with another, Neferneferuaten (Perfect is the Goodness of the Aten). By the ninth year of his reign, Akhenaten had proscribed the old deities of Egypt, and ordered their temples to be closed, a very serious matter, for these institutions played an important part in the economic and social life of the country. The Egyptians had always worshipped many deities and been ready to add new gods to the pantheon: religious persecution was new to them.

In the sixth year of his reign, Akhenaten took up residence in his new city. There he was once supposed to have lived in connubial bliss with Nefertiti, enjoying family life with their six daughters, contemplating the Aten and receiving the adulation of his courtiers. Meantime, his preoccupation with religious affairs and his reluctance to send the Egyptian army to war was allowing the Empire, under threat from the Hittites, to slip out of his grasp. Today we know that another wife, Kiya, was part of his ménage; and may have provided him with a son, Tutankhaten (Living Image of the Aten), who would have lived with her at Akhetaten; and that Akhenaten was not quite the pacifist that some of his admirers have claimed. Although he was never presented as a great warrior king in the manner of Thutmose III, for example, he, and more surprisingly, Nefertiti (*see* p.48), were both depicted on the pylon-gateways of temples in the traditional pose of smiting the enemy, in which a king was shown in the act of bringing down a mace on the head of a foe whose hair he holds grasped in his hand. There is no suggestion, of course, that in the case of Akhenaten and Nefertiti this pose was anything other than fictional. Soldiers, and Akhenaten's own bodyguard, are much in evidence in the tomb reliefs at Akhetaten; and further evidence that the military were not banished from the presence of this supposed pacifist is attested by the number of high-ranking military men at court, notably the generals Nakhtmin and Horemheb.

Thutmose III and Amenhotep II in particular had been able to take advantage of the conditions that existed in western Asia during their reigns, when many countries and petty states in the region were weak and ripe for conquest. Only Mitanni had withstood the might of Egypt. When Amenhotep III came to the throne, the situation in western Asia had changed: Mitanni was no longer a threat to Egypt but rather its ally; and engaged in an increasingly desperate struggle to fend off the resurgent power of Assyria. The Hittites, from a land lay that lay far to the north of Egypt, were also becoming more territorially ambitious. They avoided direct conflict with Egypt, but during the reign of Akhenaten the Hittite King, Suppiluliuma, adopted a policy of fomenting rebellion and intrigue among the petty princelings of Syria-Palestine. Although Amenhotep III and his son were not much given to the pursuit of war, one must be fair to them and say that probably only another Thutmose III could have dealt with the situation.

Some four years or so after Akhenaten's move to his new city, Amenhotep III seems to have paid his son a visit, an event that is perhaps commemorated on a sandstone stele that was found in the house of Panehsy (*see* p.82) in Akhetaten. On the stele, a noticeably corpulent Amenhotep III is depicted slumped on a throne, with an enthroned Tiye beside him (**20**). Out of deference to the Aten, the two *cartouches* carved above the King's head both contain his throne name, Nebmaatre, thus avoiding the use of the name Amun in the Aten's own city. The real importance of the stele lies in the fact that on it the Aten's name is in a form that was not in use until the ninth year of Akhenaten's reign (*see* p.62), which suggests that Amenhotep III, though ailing, was still alive into, and perhaps beyond, the tenth regnal year. Some scholars maintain that the stele was in fact designed for use in the cult of the dead king, but if this were so then one would expect Amenhotep III to appear in the form of a statue, not sitting alongside Tiye with both of them shown as living beings.

The twelfth year of Akhenaten's reign was momentous, not least because it may have

20. *Amenhotep III and Queen Tiye: shrine stele, sandstone (British Museum)*

been the year in which his father died. No record of this appears anywhere; but in two tombs in the northern cliffs at Akhetaten are scenes that are to be found nowhere else in Egypt. The tombs belong to Huya, who replaced Kheruef (*see* p.38) as Tiye's Steward, and Meryre, Superintendent of the Household of Queen Nefertiti (*see* p.88). The scenes are dated very precisely to Year 12, second month of Winter, eighth day. In Huya's tomb it Akhenaten and Nefertiti are borne in a carrying chair to the Hall of Foreign Tribute. In Meryre's tomb the royal couple are depicted enthroned in the Hall of Foreign Tribute receiving in audience men in foreign dress, 'the rulers of foreign lands' according to inscriptions attached to the scenes, bringing exotic gifts from all corners of the then-known world. Early Egyptologists called this event a durbar, after the Hindi word referring to a reception at the court of an Indian ruler; and it is often presented as Akhenaten pretending that the Egyptian Empire was still bringing the customary tribute to him in spite of his neglect of it.

It is possible, however, to interpret these scenes differently. H.W. Fairman was of the opinion that they represented the record of a great reception held in honour of Akhenaten's accession as sole ruler of Egypt, 12 years after his father associated him on the throne with him, and show Akhenaten receiving homage not only from foreign nations but also from his Egyptian subjects. In support of this view Fairman pointed out that the two scenes feature young men running, dancing, clapping hands, wrestling and stick-fencing, activities associated with joyous occasions such as jubilees. Fairman's theory is reinforced by a letter[39] sent by Tushratta, King of Mitanni, to Naphurureya (*i.e.* the Babylonian/Akkadian version of Akhenaten's throne name, Neferkheperure), telling of how he wept on the day that he heard of Amenhotep III's death, sitting unmoving throughout the night, neither meat nor drink giving him any pleasure. He goes on to say:

> I was full of sorrow ... if only my brother whom I loved and who loved me could live again! But when Naphurureya, the mighty son of Nibhurreya (Amenhotep III) by Tiye, his Wife-in-Chief, wrote to me saying, 'I have succeeded to the kingly office' then I said, 'Nibhurreya is not dead: Naphurureya ... has taken his place and he will not allow anything to be changed from what it was formerly.'

Tushratta does not neglect to add to this touching missive a reminder that 'in my brother's land gold is as plentiful as dust' in the hope of gifts to come. The letter clearly refers to Akhenaten's accession to the throne, and is one of the very few on which an Egyptian scribe has recorded the date of its arrival: Year 12. The scribe also recorded the fact that the letter arrived in Akhetaten at a time when Akhenaten was in Waset — presumably to attend to the burial of his father in the Valley of the Kings.

A happier event in the twelfth year of Akhenaten's reign was the inauguaration of a special sort of temple that had been built for Tiye in Akhetaten. Called a *šwyt-r'*, (lit: shade of the sun) or Sunshade-temple, it was a small, open-sided pavilion set beside a pool within a walled rectangular area planted with trees and flowers to form a shady garden. This type of temple, the most famous of which was the Maru-Aten (*see* p.58 and p.84), was unique to Akhetaten, and was closely connected with the female members of the royal family, who visited their Sunshade-temples daily to be rejuvenated by the rays of the sun — the Aten. A relief depicting Akhenaten leading his mother into her new temple was carved in the tomb of Huya, Tiye's Steward. So was a scene of Huya officiating at a banquet (*see* p.88) attended by Akhenaten, Tiye and Nefertiti, at which Tiye was accompanied by her daughter, Beketaten, and Nefertiti by Meretaten and another, unnamed, daughter. The banquet was perhaps held to celebrate the inauguration of what was, in effect, a solarium.

The fact that Huya, Tiye's Steward, had his tomb at Akhetaten would suggest that he had lived there; and if this were the case then naturally Tiye would have lived there also, if only intermittently. By the fourteenth year of her son's reign, she had died and been buried in the Royal Tomb at Akhetaten, although it seems that eventually her body was removed to her husband's tomb in the Valley of the Kings. It was not left in peace there, however, for the tomb was empty when the modern excavators discovered it. The mummy of a woman found in a side chamber of Amenhotep II's tomb and for years known as the Elder Lady (**21**) has been identified as Tiye.[40] This was done by comparing the measurements obtained from a cephalogram, or lateral head radiogram, of her cranium with those of ten other female mummies known to be connected with the Eighteenth-Dynasty royal family. It was found that the closest match to the Elder Lady was

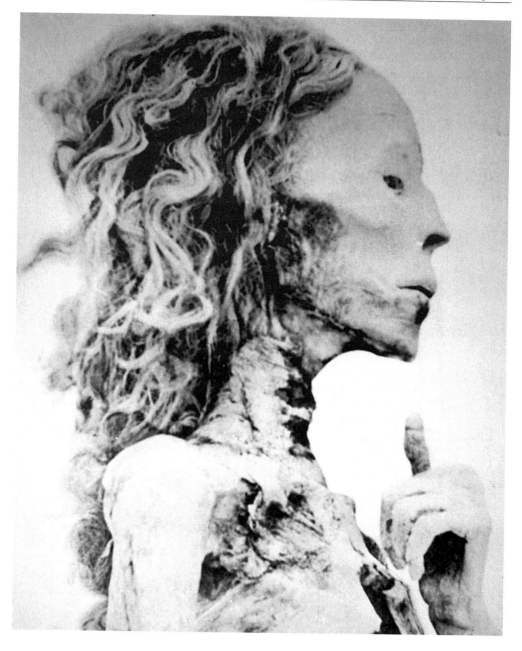

21.   *'The Elder Lady' (side chamber, tomb of Amenhotep II, Luxor)*

22. *Tiye's hair from a locket found in the tomb of Tutankhamun (Cairo Museum)*

Thuya, known to be the mother of Tiye. The identification was confirmed by taking control samples of hair, together with strands of hair obtained from the head of the Elder Lady, and subjecting them to ion etching and scanning electron microprobe analysis. The same procedures were also used to examine hairs found in the tomb of Tutankhamun in a box (*see* p.127) on which an inscription states that the tress of hair (**22**) inside belonged to Queen Tiye. On the basis that hair is as peculiar to an individual as his or her fingerprints a match was made. If the identification is correct, then Tiye died in her late forties, her hair still long, naturally curly and dark brown. She was reburied in the tomb of Amenhotep II, possibly in company with her daughter, Sitamun, and her elder son, Thutmose (*see* p.29), who had, like their mother, once been buried in the tomb of Amenhotep III.

23.   *Death of Princess Meketaten. Drawing of a relief in the royal tomb, Tell el-Amarna [from N. Davies, The Rock Tombs of el-Amarna, 1903-8]*

Within a year or so of the inauguration of Tiye's Sunshade-temple, at the latest by the fourteenth year of Akhenaten's reign, Tiye's granddaughter, Meketaten had, like her grandmother, died and been buried in the Royal Tomb at Akhetaten. A relief (**23**) in the suite of rooms in the tomb allocated to Meketaten shows the young princess lying on a bier, her grieving parents leaning over her. Above this relief is one that depicts Akhenaten and Nefertiti grieving, presumably over the body of Meketaten, although that part of the relief is damaged; and behind the royal couple a female figure carrying a baby, whose father is presumed to have been Akhenaten. In the absence of inscriptions in these reliefs it has been suggested[41] that they in fact depict the death of Queen Kiya; and some are reluctant to accept that they represent Meketaten's death in childbirth because she would have been only eleven or twelve years old at the time. But many girls of that age are perfectly capable of bearing a child; and Meketaten's sisters, Meretaten and Ankhesenpaaten, bore children at a very young age. Whoever's death is depicted in these reliefs, Akhenaten is movingly portrayed with one hand clasped to his brow, blindly groping behind him with the other to seek the comfort of Nefertiti's touch.

Many have explained these unions between Akhenaten and his daughters as acts of desperation by a man driven by Nefertiti's inability to give him a son to marry his daughters in an attempt to sire a son by them. This view of Akhenaten and Nefertiti seems to have been much influenced by the endeavours of Henry the Eighth to beget a son to inherit the throne of England, in pursuit of which he married six wives. Unlike the King of Egypt, of course, Henry could not have more than one wife at a time and had to pursue a variety of stratagems from divorce to beheading to rid himself of wives who failed to give him sons. Akhenaten, however, was not faced with Henry's problem regarding a son and heir: according to ancient Egyptian laws of royal inheritance, it would have been perfectly feasible for him to have married one of his daughters to a promising young man who would thereby eventually gain the throne of Egypt. In any case, he may have had sons, even by Nefertiti. The fact that sons are not mentioned at Akhetaten is consistent with the Eighteenth-Dynasty practice of naming and depicting royal daughters whilst allowing their brothers to remain almost invisible.[42]

The death of Meketaten was closely followed by that of Kiya. At the same time, Meretaten became her father's wife, with the title of Queen-in-Chief. It was once assumed that Nefertiti either died in the thirteenth year of Akhenaten's reign,[43] for her name disappears from the records after that date; or fell out of favour for some reason. Reasons proposed have been her jealousy of Meretaten; or her enthusiasm for Atenism outlasting that of Akhenaten. In support of the former reason it was pointed out that inscriptions in the Maru-Aten, supposed to be Nefertiti's Sunshade-temple, had been altered, with Meretaten's name being cut over that of her mother; but it is now generally agreed that the Maru-Aten did not belong to Nefertiti at all but to Kiya, and was adapted as the Sunshade-temple of Queen Meretaten after Kiya's death. Disagreement over the Aten was said to have resulted in Nefertiti being banished to the Northern Palace at Akhetaten, which, when excavated, yielded objects bearing the names of Nefertiti, Tutankhaten and Ankhesenpaaten, Nefertiti's daughter who became Tutankhaten's wife. No excavation report was ever published, but H.W. Fairman was certain that no object had been found bearing the names of Nefertiti and Tutankhaten together. There is no proof therefore that the three ever lived together in the Northern Palace.

A reasonable hypothesis, admittedly on scanty evidence, that has recently been put forward to explain the disappearance of Nefertiti's name is that, simply, she changed it.[44] The evidence comes from the tomb of Pere[45] in the necropolis of Waset in which a draughtsman named Pawah sketched a prayer to Amun, and dated his *graffito* to 'Regnal Year 3 under the King of Upper and Lower Egypt, Ankhkheperure, beloved of the Aten, the Son of Re, Neferneferuaten, beloved of Waenre (Akhenaten)'. The name Neferneferuaten is one associated above all with Nefertiti; but as she had not adopted the name until the fifth year of Akhenaten's reign, the theory is that the date written in the *graffito* refers to the third year of the reign of a king called Ankhkheperure Neferneferuaten. If this is so, then the second name, Neferneferuaten, in conjunction with its epithet, 'beloved of Waenre', must surely identify 'King Ankhkheperure' as Nefertiti. She would not have been the first woman to call herself King: some 140 years previously, Hatshepsut had referred to herself as the 'female king'. However, the name 'Ankhkheperure' is known to be the throne name of Smenkhkare, Akhenaten's successor; and one *graffito* does not amount to fact. Pawah may simply have confused the royal names.

It has also been suggested[46] that Nefertiti as 'King Ankhkheperure' was associated on the throne with Akhenaten in the 13th year of his reign. This would mean that from then on Akhenaten reigned in Akhetaten only while Nefertiti moved to Waset, there to rule the rest of Egypt, leaving her eldest daughter, Meretaten, to take her place at Akhenaten's side. On the death of Akhenaten, Nefertiti relinquished her position and moved back to Akhetaten where, two or three years later, she died and was buried in the Royal Tomb. Whether or not the hypotheses outlined above are correct, the name of Nefertiti did disappear from the records in the last few years of Akhenaten's reign, to be replaced by that of Meretaten. She, however, did not act as her father's Queen-in-Chief for long before being handed on to his chosen successor, Smenkhkare (*see* Chapter 6), and replaced as her father's Queen-in-Chief by her younger sister, Ankhesenpaaten. The unfortunate Meretaten was destined to have a short married life with her new husband and died within a year or so of her marriage to him.

Towards the end of his reign, Akhenaten unleashed a furious campaign against the Aten's rival deities. The temples of Amun had been closed in his ninth regnal year in what was perhaps less an act of religious zeal and more one of economic necessity. Once the temples had been closed down, their income and the revenues from their vast estates could be redirected to Akhenaten, who needed extra sources of revenue to build his new city and to maintain the lavish daily offerings that were made to the Aten. In his final years Akhenaten moved against other deities, and throughout Egypt their temples were closed down, their statues were destroyed and their names expunged from inscriptions. Even the *cartouches* of his father did not escape attention, the element of his name bearing the hated syllable Amun being chiselled out wherever it appeared. Such excesses were in contrast to the earlier days of the reign, when Akhenaten had tolerated the old deities — with good cause, since temples played a vital role in the economic and social life of the Egyptians. The reason for this untoward and destructive campaign is not known, but it may have been political rather than religious, triggered by an attempt to divert attention away from a worsening situation in western Asia.

At the beginning of Akhenaten's reign, the Hittite king, Suppiluliuma, had taken the opportunity of driving a wedge between Egypt and its ally, Mitanni. He tempted Akhenaten into an alliance and then moved to attack Mitanni's possessions in northern Syria, notably Nuhasse, prompting the ruler of Nuhasse, Abdu-nirari, to send a desperate appeal to the King of Egypt, to the effect that:

> When Manahpiya (Menkheperre *i.e.* Thutmose III), the King of Egypt, your forebear, made Taku, my forebear, king in Nuhasse, he anointed his head with oil and spoke as follows: Whosoever the King of Egypt has made a king, let no one [depose?].[47]

But Akhenaten left Abdu-nirari to his fate.

Throughout Akhenaten's reign, although there was no direct confrontation between Egypt and the Hittites, Suppululiuma encouraged Egypt's vassal rulers to quarrel among themselves — not that they needed much encouragement, being prone to anarchy and ever ready to indulge in petty jealousies and back-biting. Egypt's most loyal ally seems to have been Ribaddi of Byblos, who sent over 50 letters[48] to Akhenaten seeking help against Abdiashirta of Amor, and later against Abdiashirta's son, Aziru. Ribaddi warned that 'Abdiashirta is a cur and he is aiming to capture all the cities of the king'. He claimed that

Akhenaten's inaction was allowing Byblos 'to go out of his hand', all for the lack of a pitifully small amount of aid: just 20 pairs of horses and 300 men, which would have enabled him to hold the city.

It is clear from the Amarna Letters (*see* p.135) that Aziru corresponded with Akhenaten's minister of protocol, the Chamberlain, Tutu, whom he called Dudu, 'mouthpiece of the entire land'. It is possible that Tutu favoured Aziru and therefore arranged matters so that Akhenaten did not receive all of the letters sent to him; but, finally, Akhenaten sent a warning to Aziru:

> If for any reason whatsoever you prefer to do evil, if you plot to do evil, treacherous things, then you, together with your entire family, shall die by the axe of the King. Therefore perform your duty to the King, your lord, and you will live. You know that the King does not fail when he rages against all of Canaan.[49]

Akhenaten eventually summoned Aziru to Egypt to give an account of himself;[50] and, reluctantly, Aziru came. But perhaps this was a last desperate attempt on the part of Akhenaten to assert his authority over at least one wily and treacherous vassal.

Akhenaten may have distracted attention from trouble in the Empire by initiating action at home against the deities of Egypt, thus reversing the age-old device whereby a ruler with problems at home distracts his people by means of a war against a foreign enemy; but the explanations for Akhenaten's behaviour may, of course, lie on a more domestic and personal level. The final years of his reign were marked by the deaths of many of those he loved, perhaps driving him to excesses that he had so far resisted. They may even have sapped him of the will to live, for at the beginning of the 18th year of his reign, at the age of perhaps 35 or so, he died and was either buried with his beloved Nefertiti in the Royal Tomb at Akhetaten, or perhaps waited for her to join him there.

4. The King and the Aten

The religion of the Aten

The cult of the sun was very ancient in Egypt: its symbolism could be understood by everybody even if, in its remoteness and intangibility, the sun was less appealing to ordinary people on a personal level than the old animal deities. It was worshipped in different forms: in the shape of a falcon as Horus and Horakhty; in the form of a divine scarab-beetle as Khepri, the young sun god; in the shape of an old man leaning on a stick as Atum, the most ancient deity, who represented the setting sun; and in the form of the midday sun as Re. There had always been an incipient monotheism in Egypt, for the Egyptians were accustomed to having local gods who were syncretized with others when political considerations dictated it. Because every local god in Egypt was identified in the minds of his followers with the state god, in essence this meant that each Egyptian could chose to worship one god made up of his own local god or gods and whichever deity was the state god of the time. In practice, this did not happen, for the Egyptians were essentially polytheistic, allotting different functions to different gods. However, in the Eighteenth Dynasty, the sun god, Re, with whom it had become the custom for lesser deities to syncretize, had almost become the theoretically possible 'one god'; and even the powerful Amun was known as Amen-Re.

Both Amenhotep III and Amenhotep IV identified themselves with the sun. As we have seen, Amenhotep III was the first king to have a temple and a cult dedicated to himself in his own lifetime; and at Soleb and Sedeinga, where he and his son were both depicted offering to their deified selves, the sun god was epitomized in the person of the King. It had long been the custom in Egypt for a king's death to be described as his being raised up into the sky, there to unite with the sun's disk. Amenhotep III did not wait until his death for his transfiguration, but achieved it through the celebration of his first *heb-sed*, through which he was supposedly transformed into the living Re-Horakhty. Until this time, it was believed that Amun in combination with Re daily transmitted his life-giving force through the rays of the sun. After Amenhotep III's transformation it was Re in combination with Horakhty who performed this service to mankind. It could, of course, have simply been Amenhotep III's hubris that led him to claim such a transfiguration; but if this were so, he could simply have identified himself with Amen-Re. By choosing Re-Horakhty as his vehicle, he excluded Amun, some think as a deliberate exercise by which he countered the threat posed to his throne by the power of the priesthood of Amun; and emphasised the downgrading of Amun by favouring rival deities, including yet another sun god, the Aten.

The word *aten* had been in use in Egypt for over 500 years before Amenhotep III came to the throne, the earliest example of its use so far found being in one of the magical inscriptions painted inside Twelfth-Dynasty (1963–1786BC) coffins. In the great narrative tale of the same period known as *The Story of Sinuhe*, a king is described as dying and being 'united with the sun'; and in the same story a letter sent by Sinuhe to his king contains the phrase 'the sun rises at your pleasure'. In both cases, the word used for 'sun' is *aten* rather than the more usual *re*. The chief source for *The Story of Sinuhe*, Papyrus Berlin 10499, uses the word *aten* in the first example with the sign for god appended to it, while a secondary source, written on an ostracon (a piece from a broken clay pot now in the Ashmolean Museum in Oxford), uses the god sign for the second example also. It seems certain, therefore, that the Egyptians had a sun god called 'Aten' in the Twelfth Dynasty if not before.

In the Eighteenth Dynasty, possibly as early as the reign of Thutmose III, the Aten became a recognized member of the Egyptian pantheon, representing the physical power of the sun's disk and its omnipresent and life-giving properties. Thutmose IV issued a large commemorative scarab, now in the British Museum,[51] on which the Aten appears as a war-god who goes in front of the king to bring him victory. In the reign of Amenhotep III, the Aten was established as a god of Empire, and at the same time became ever closer to the King. One of the royal epithets was *Tekhen-Aten* (Radiance of the Aten), a term found also as the name of a company of the Royal Bodyguard, a town, a lake, and the king's State Barge (*see* p.26).

It had been the custom to depict the Aten as a man with the head of a falcon surmounted by a sun's disk — not dissimilar from Re-Horakhty. Early in Amenhotep IV's reign, however, the iconography of Aten underwent a change. The inspiration for this change perhaps dates back to a stele, erected in front of the Sphinx at Giza on behalf of Amenhotep II, on which the sun is depicted with two arms descending from its disk to embrace the royal *cartouche*. The Aten of Amenhotep IV (**24**) is represented as a solar disk with many rays depending from it, each ray terminating in a hand, with some of the hands holding *ankh*-signs (☥), symbolizing the giving of life.

From the fifth year of Akhenaten's reign, when he changed his name from Amenhotep to Akhenaten, great emphasis was placed on the kingship of the Aten. The Aten's so-called didactic, or instructive name, which elaborated on the basic appellation Aten in order to reflect what was perceived to be the true character of the god, was divided into two parts, each inscribed inside a *cartouche* as though he were an earthly king. The Aten was given regnal years which were identical with those of Akhenaten; together, the two kings, Akhenaten and the Aten, or the two gods, the Aten and Akhenaten, celebrated their joint *heb-sed* or jubilee. From the fifth year, Akhenaten and the Aten were indivisible, and the cult of divine kingship, long since a part of Egyptian culture, was taken to extremes.

In the ninth year of his reign, Akhenaten made a change in the didactic name of the Aten. The earlier form of the name reads: 'Long live Re-Horakhty who rejoices on the horizon'; followed by: 'In his name of Shu who is the Aten'. The later form of the name reads: 'Long live Re ruler of the two horizons who rejoices on the horizon'; followed by: 'In his name of Re the father who has appeared as the Aten'. The later name reflects a tightening-up of the theology: since the first element of the earlier name contained the

24.   The Aten, door jamb from Tell el-Amarna (Cairo Museum)

name of the god Horakhty (meaning Horus of the Two Horizons *i.e.* the places where the sun rises and sets), the Horus element was dropped and replaced by the word 'ruler'. In the second element Shu, normally the god of air but here identified as a sun god, has been replaced by Re, who clearly was considered a more pure form of the sun than Shu.

Thus the religion of Akhenaten, expressed in simplest terms, was a form of solar monotheism in which the sun was worshipped in the shape of the sun's disk or *aten*. Attempts have been made to prove that Atenism was inspired by western Asiatic and Semitic monotheistic beliefs, possibly introduced into Egypt by the Mitannian princesses Gilukhipa and Tadukhipa; but there were no monotheistic movements in western Asia at the time, certainly no Hebrew monotheism in the modern sense, and even more certainly no solar cults that remotely resembled Atenism. The origins of Atenism were purely Egyptian.

It is clear that Akhenaten did not invent the Aten, but he did develop and elaborate the concept. We do not know his motivation for doing so and can only theorize on whether the impetus for his Atenism was religious or political: but it was expressed in art that has its own unique appeal; and poetically as the universal cherishing of all living things. After the fifth year of Akhenaten's reign the Aten was represented pictorially by the image of a sun-disk with descending rays, each ending in a hand. Some of the hands hold *ankh*-signs; and, although the Aten was regarded as the source of life of the whole of creation, it is instructive that these symbols of life are only ever offered to the King and Queen, and occasionally to other members of the royal family. Atenism was a very exclusive religion confined to the royal family, with the King as the only mediator between man and god; and it is clear that Atenism was not so much a monotheism as a henotheism, that is, the worship of one god as the special deity of one's family. That family prided itself on living 'according to Maat', a word that is often translated as 'Truth', its literal meaning, but that is perhaps best interpreted as an orderly, well-regulated existence.

The fullest statement of Akhenaten's faith is found in a beautiful hymn carved on the west wall of Ay's tomb at Akhetaten. Although the hymn was written for, some say by, Akhenaten, in Ay's tomb it has been adapted for the tomb-owner to recite; and shorter versions of it are to be found in other tombs at Akhetaten. The first section of the hymn decribes the universal splendour and power of the Aten:

> How beautiful is your appearance on the horizon of heaven,
> 0 Living Aten who creates life.
> When you rise on the eastern horizon
> You fill every land with your beauty.
> You are beautiful and great, gleaming high over every land.
> Your rays, they embrace the earth
> To the furthest limits of what you have created.
> You are Re; you conquer them all,
> Making them subject to your beloved son.
> You are far away yet your rays are upon earth;
> You are on the faces of men yet your paths are unknown.

1   Amen-Re and the goddess Mut: façade of Ramesses III temple, Karnak (see p.19)

2   *Temple of Amun, Karnak: processional way (see p.20)*

3   *Senwosret kiosk, Karnak (see p.30)*

4   *Luxor Temple (see p.30)*

5   *Northern Colossus of Memnon, Luxor (see p.32)*

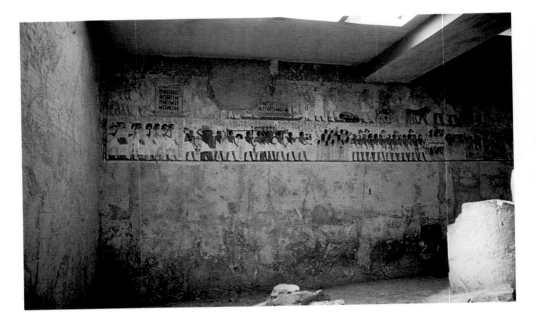

6   *Tomb of Ramose, Luxor: wall painting of his funeral procession (see p.38)*

7   *Princesses Neferneferuaten-Tasherit and Neferneferure. From a painting by Nina de Garis Davies (Ashmolean Museum, Oxford) (see p.49)*

8   *Yuya: head of mummy (Cairo Museum)* *(see p.42)*

9 *Nefertiti: bust, painted limestone (Ägyptisches Museum, Berlin) (see pp.48, 99 &138)*

10   *Akhenaten: upper half of sandstone colossus from the destroyed Temple of theAten, Karnak (Cairo Museum) (see p.72)*

11   Boundary Stele A, Tuna el-Gebel. (see p.79)

12   North Palace, Tell el-Amarna (see p.85)

13   *Sarcophagus of Akhenaten: fragment carved with head of Nefertiti (Ägyptisches Museum,Berlin) (see p.92)*

14   *Bust of an unidentifed Amarna princess, painted limestone (Musée du Louvre, Paris) (see p.93)*

15   *Head of an unidentified Amarna princess from workshop of the sculptor, Thutmose, Tell el-Amarna, brown quartzite (Ägyptisches Museum, Berlin) (see p.99)*

16   *Meretaten offering Smenkhkare the fruit of a mandrake (a symbol of love, its root used in aphrodisiacs), painted limestone (Ägyptisches Museum, Berlin) (see p.105)*

17   *Wall painting, North Palace at Tell el-Amarna (Cairo Museum) (see p.85)*

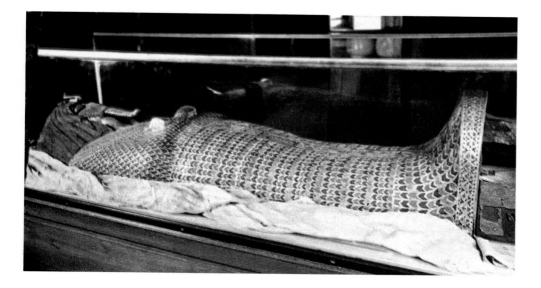

18   *Tomb 55, Valley of the Kings, Luxor: coffin (Cairo Museum) (see p.110)*

19   *Tutankhamun: throne (Cairo Museum) (see p.126)*

20   *Tutankhamun: gold shrine (Cairo Museum) (see p.126)*

21   *Tutankhamun: gold funerary mask (Cairo Museum) (see p.125)*

22   *Tutankhamun: burial chamber: Ay (on right)performs funerary rites for Tutankhamun (see p.128)*

The second section describes mankind's condition at night:

> When you set on the western horizon
> The earth is in darkness in the manner of the dead
> Who sleep in their chambers,
> Their heads covered
> And no eye seeing its fellow.
> All their possessions could be stolen,
> Even though they are under their heads,
> And they would know it not.

The third section describes the condition of animals at night:

> Every lion comes forth from its den
> And all snakes are ready to bite,
> For darkness is the only illumination
> And the earth is silent,
> For he who created it rests in his horizon.

The fourth section describes mankind's condition during the day:

> Day dawns when you rise on the horizon.
> You shine by day as Aten
> Who dispels the darkness.
> When you send forth your sunbeams
> The Two Lands are festive,
> The people awake and jump to their feet
> For you have roused them.
> Their bodies are washed
> And they don their clothing;
> Their arms are upraised in adoration at your appearance.
> And the whole world goes about its work.

The fifth section describes the condition of animals and plants during the day:

> All cattle rest in their pastures;
> Trees and vegetation are verdant;
> Birds fly up from their nests, their wings raised in adoration of you.
> Goats all jump on their feet and
> Everything that flys and flutters lives when you shine upon it.

The sixth section speaks about watery things:

> Boats sail upstream, and downstream likewise,

And all roads are open because you have arisen.
The fish in the river leap before your face,
And your rays are in the midst of the great green sea.

The seventh section speaks about creation:

You are the one who causes women to be fecund,
Who makes seed in men,
Who gives life to a son in his mother's womb,
Who soothes him with whatever dries his tears
By acting as his nurse even in the womb,
Who gives the breath of life to everything that he has made.
When he emerges from the womb
To breathe on the day of his birth,
You open his mouth wide and supply what it needs.
The chick in the egg cheeps whilst still in the shell
For you have given it breath therein so that it might live.
You make for it the strength
With which it breaks it, namely the egg,
And it emerges from the egg at the appointed hour
To cheep and run on its feet as soon as it issues therefrom.

In the eighth section the universal creation of the Aten is extolled:

How manifold are your works
That are hidden from the face of mankind,
0 Sole God, who is like none other.
You made the earth according to your will alone:
Men and women, cattle and all beasts,
Everything on earth that walks upon feet,
Everything above that flies with its wings,
Foreign lands, Syria, Kush
And the land of Egypt.
You set everyone in his place and supply his needs,
Everyone has his provisions
And his allotted life-span.
Their tongues are diverse in speech
And their appearance likewise;
Their skins are different for you have differentiated the peoples.

The ninth section speaks of the watering of the earth both in Egypt and in foreign lands:

It is in the Underworld that you make the Nile
And bring it forth at your will

So that mankind might live.
For you have made them for yourself,
O Lord of all, who grows weary on their behalf,
O Lord of every land, who shines upon them.
All distant lands, you make whatever they need to live on.
You have set a Nile in the sky
So that it may descend for them
And make waves upon the mountains like the sea,
So that their fields may be watered in their townships.
How marvellous are your schemes, 0 Lord of Eternity.
The heavenly Nile is what you have created for foreign peoples
And for all the game in the desert that walk upon feet;
But the (real) Nile comes forth from the Underworld for Egypt.

The tenth section speaks of the seasons:

Your rays nourish every field and when you rise, they live and flourish for you.
It is in order to sustain all that you have created that you have
made the seasons:
Winter to cool them
And the heat (of Summer) so that they may taste you.

The eleventh section speaks of the Aten's universal dominion:

You have made the sky afar off in order to shine therein
And to see all that you have made,
You alone, rising in your form of the living Aten,
Appearing and shining, far off, yet close at hand.
From out of yourself alone you have made myriad forms —
Cities, towns, fields, roads and river.
All eyes see you before them,
For you are Aten the daylight over the earth.
Even when you are done, your eye (still) exists
For you have created their forms.
If you did not see [rest of line damaged].

The twelfth and final section speaks of the revelation of the Aten and his works to the
King:

You are in my heart,
There is none other that knows you
Except your son Neferkheperure Waenre,[52]
Whom you have acquainted with your plans and your power.
The earth exists in your hand, just as you have made it.

When you rise, it lives: when you set, it dies.
You yourself are Lifetime
And it is by you that men live.
Eyes gaze upon your beauty until you set,
But when you set in the west, all work is laid aside,
When you rise again, you make [lost] grow for the king.
Movement has been in every leg
Since you founded the earth.
You have raised up (its inhabitants)
For your son who came forth from your flesh —
The King of Upper and Lower Egypt, who lives on Truth,
The Lord of the Two Lands, Neferkheperure Waenre,
The Son of Re, who lives on Truth,
Lord of Diadems, Akhenaten, whose life is long;
And for the Great Royal Wife, his beloved,
The Mistress of the Two Lands, Neferneferuaten
Nefertiti, may she live and grow young for ever and ever.[53]

Although there is little likelihood that the Hymn to the Aten directly influenced the writing of the Hebrew Psalmist, several passages find an echo in the 104th Psalm, in particular Verses 20-24 and 29-30:

Thou makest darkness, and it is night, wherein all the beasts of
the forest do creep forth.
The young lions roar after their prey and seek their meat from
God.
The sun ariseth, they gather themselves together and lay them
down in their dens.
Man goeth forth unto his work and to his labour until the
evening.
O Lord, how manifold are thy works! In wisdom hast thou
made them all: the earth is full of thy riches.
Thou hidest thy face, they are troubled: thou takest away
their breath, they die, and return to their dust.
Thou sendest forth thy spirit, they are created: and thou
renewest the face of the earth.[54]

Even before the move to Akhetaten, the Aten had become a trinity consisting of Re — the primordial god, the demi-urge — as the father; the Aten — visible to man in the form of the sun's disk — as the physical expression the father; and Akhenaten, the physical manifestation on earth of both of them. Akhenaten was the son of Re, the son of the Aten; but at the same time, he was the father of both, and further, he was both Re and Aten. This was the trinity that was at the same time a unity that was worshipped at Akhetaten; and the fact that the chief officiant in its temples was called the High Priest of Akhenaten is a

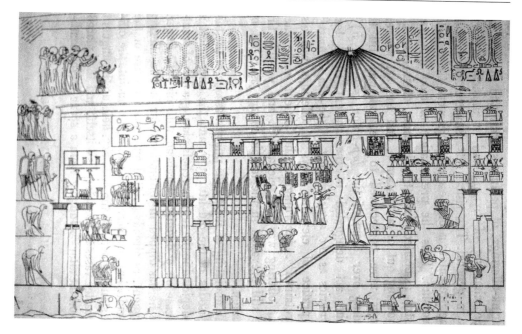

25.   *The Per Aten Temple. Drawing by N. Davies* (see *caption to text photograph 23) of a relief in the tomb of Panehsy, Tell el-Amarna*

clear indication that it was the King himself who was worshipped in them. It was only the King and the royal family who were ever officially depicted worshipping the Aten. The ordinary Egyptian was expected to worship him through the medium of the King; and to accept Akhenaten as his personal god.

The temples of the Aten

From the earliest years of Akhenaten's reign and possibly in the later years of his father's, temples dedicated to the Aten appear to have been constructed in most of the major towns of Egypt, within the precincts of already-existing temples belonging to other deities. Finally however, with the building of Akhetaten, Akhenaten was able to claim a site that had not been contaminated by any other god. The new temple, the *Per Aten* (The House of the Aten), a great enclosure some 730m by 230, lay on the eastern edge of the Central City (**25**). It contained two distinct stone structures, one of which was called the *Gem Pa Aten*, ([The Place of] He Who Found the Aten), a long, narrow building measuring 210m by 32, with a front section called the *Per Hai* (The House of Rejoicing). In some ways the layout of the *Gem Pa Aten* was traditional, with a monumental entrance gateway, or pylon, leading to an open courtyard. But whereas the areas leading from the courtyard of a conventional ancient Egyptian temple consisted of several enclosed and darkened halls culminating in a sanctuary in which the cult-statue of the temple deity was housed, the halls in the *Gem Pa Aten* were open to the sky, and seem to have been crammed with small stone or brick offering tables. There was no need for a cult-statue of the Aten, for the Aten was its own image and was worshipped from the temple, not within it.

The second structure within the *Per Aten* is now known as the Sanctuary. It seems to have been inspired by the Sun Temples built in the Fifth Dynasty (*c.*2498–2345BC) at Abu Ghurob, near Inebhedj. Each of these consisted of a raised platform upon which was placed a *benben*-stone, the pyramid-shaped fetish that represented the island created by the sun god, Atum, at the beginning of the world. At Akhetaten the *benben*-stone was replaced by a stele, not in itself an object of worship, on which was carved a representation of Akhenaten and Nefertiti worshipping the Aten. The buildings within the precinct of the *Per Aten* were surrounded by a rectangular enclosure wall. Set into its north-eastern end was a large altar which, judging by its name — the Hall of Foreign Tribute — was the place where offerings supposedly from foreign lands were laid. There were several other temples and shrines at Akhetaten, the most important of which lay some 500m to the south of the *Per Aten* and was known as the *Hwt Aten*, (the Mansion of the Aten) (**26**). The temples, all smaller than the Great Temple or *Per Aten*, were similar to each other and all arranged so that the focal point of worship was upwards towards the sun's disk.

The daily liturgy in the temples of the Aten differed from that in traditional temples, where the worship of a god or goddess reflected in many ways the fact that a priest was a servant in his or her house. In these temples, therefore, the daily ritual began with the awakening of the deity, represented by a cult-statue, washing, anointing and dressing him, and presenting him with his morning meal, which then reverted to the priests of the temple. There were no cult-statues in the Aten temples however, so that all the pre-toilet and toilet episodes of the daily ritual[55] were abolished. Worship of the Aten was performed mainly by singing hymns while presenting lavish offerings of food and drink, flowers and perfume. The ritual acts accompanying these presentations were similar to those in the old temples and consisted of burning incense and pouring libations, and consecrating the offerings in the traditional way by touching them with a special baton called the *hrp* (*see* Glossary). There was no statue to anoint, but unguent was placed upon the altars.

Ritual in the *Per Aten* began with the King and Queen entering the temple precinct where they presented offerings laid on altars in front of the pylon-gateway of the *Gem Pa Aten*, consecrating them with *hrp*-batons whilst their daughters rattled sistra (*see* Glossary). Then, having passed through the pylon-gateway and through the courtyard, the King and Queen mounted the steps of the high altar, on top of which were set out offerings of meat, poultry, vegetables and flowers surmounted by three open pans of burning incense. During this time, priests were placing offerings upon the altars in the courtyard, including parts of the many oxen that had been sacrificed in honour of Akhenaten. While the King and Queen were officiating at the high altar, music was played, not least by the princesses rattling their sistra; and by four male chanters who intoned hymns during the ceremony. A group of female musicians performed in the outer court but were never allowed beyond it; and the same stricture applied to the temple choir, which was made up of blind singers accompanied by a blind harper who performed at intervals during the day, every day.

In the traditional temples it was the king who was in theory the chief officiant in ceremonies, and temple reliefs always depict him performing the rituals, although in practice his place was taken by the temples' high priests. At Akhetaten, Akhenaten was his

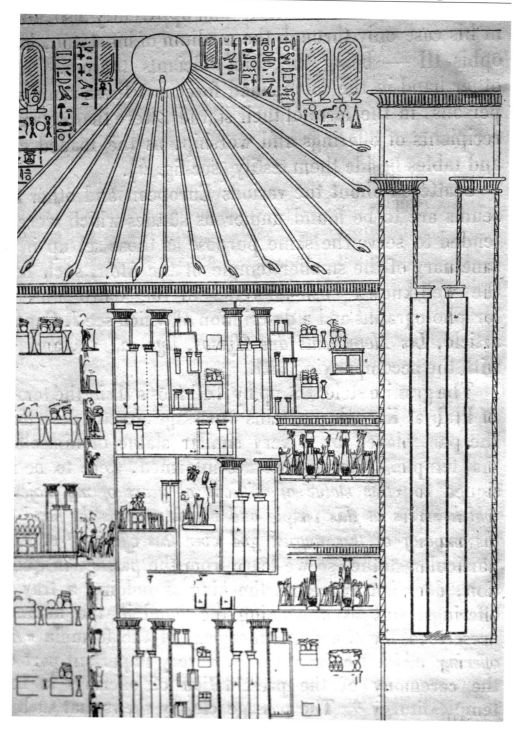

26. *The Ḥwt Aten Temple. Drawing by N. Davies (see caption to text photograph 23) of a relief in the tomb of Huya, Tell el-Amarna*

own High Priest, but it is clear that Nefertiti played as active a part in temple ritual as the King. In countless reliefs she is shown participating with Akhenaten in offering scenes, apparently standing behind him, although this may be because of the dictates of two-dimensional representation and she may, in real life, have stood beside him. Other female members of the royal family, from the Queens Tiye and Kiya, to Meretaten and the other princesses, featured prominently not only in religious ceremonies but also on state occasions. At no other period of Egyptian history have women played roles comparable to those undertaken by the royal women of Akhetaten.

At Waset, Nefertiti's role in the worship of the Aten was even more prominent. The Temple of the Aten was built to the east of the Temple of Amun; but in front of the Amun temple a series of pillars, probably 12 in number, each about 2m square and 10m high, was erected. Towards its rear, a shrine called the *Ḥwt Benben* (the Mansion of the Benben), was built around an obelisk (see Glossary) that had been erected there by Thutmose IV.[56] The *Ḥwt Benben* was described as the *Gmt Pa Aten*, an appellation similar to the name given to part of the *Per Aten* at Akhetaten (see p.69) but with the addition of the letter t. The letter t feminized the participle, *gm*, thus particularizing the *Gmt Pa Aten* ([The Place of] She Who Found the Aten), to Nefertiti. Reliefs in the two structures show Nefertiti officiating alone, standing in the place normally reserved for the King before the heavily-loaded offering tables. In every scene she is accompanied either by Meretaten or, more rarely, by Meketaten or Ankhesenpaaten, her three eldest daughters, each princess shaking a sistrum; but Akhenaten is nowhere to be seen. The whole of one side of each of the pillars is taken up with a relief of Nefertiti and one of her daughters standing beneath the Aten, whose rays take up nearly two-thirds of the surface. Like the rest of the Aten Temple at Waset, the *ḥwt benben* was dismantled after Akhenaten's death; but the pillars, inevitably known today as 'Nefertiti's Pillars', survived, partially intact, inside the walls of the Second Pylon-gateway of the Amun Temple that was built around them, possibly in the reign of Tutankhamun.

Royal sculpture: art, religion or pathology?

The art of the Amarna Age is immediately recognisable because of its naturalistic style. Nowhere is this more seemingly obvious than in statues and reliefs of Akhenaten, in which the concept of living according to Truth has apparently been ruthlessly interpreted in depictions of the King which, by ancient Egyptian standards, are unflattering in the extreme. If the portrayal of Akhenaten in statues and reliefs is accurate, then he had a prognathous jaw, prominent collar bones with deep 'saltcellars', long, sinewy arms, large hands, pendulous breasts, protruding belly, fatty thighs and spindle legs. The style is evident early in Akhenaten's reign in the colossal sandstone statues[57] that once stood before the façade of the Aten Temple at Waset (**27**). The faces of these statues have hollow cheeks, thin, elongated noses and narrowly slit eyes beneath hooded lids (**colour plate 10**). Other statues from the Aten Temple represent Nefertiti: but facially these statues are carbon copies of Akhenaten's, almost making the Queen whose name means 'The Beautiful One is Present' her husband's identical twin (**28**). This phenomenon was presumably an attempt to identify her with Akhenaten as the human link with the divine

27. *Akhenaten: sandstone colossus from the destroyed Temple of the Aten, Karnak (Cairo Museum)*

28.   *Akhenaten, fragment of a relief showing his head (British Museum)*

being, the Aten; and there are instances in which Queen Kiya has been subjected to the same twinning process.

Such a marked departure from the normal convention of depicting a king in heroic mode as an athletic man in the prime of life must have been undertaken by the artist with the express permission of Akhenaten; and indeed, his Master Sculptor, Bek, claimed, that he was 'an apprentice whom the King himself instructed'.[58] Thereafter, the supposed deformities of Akhenaten, especially the prognathous jaw, bulbous hips and spindle shanks, were often reproduced in representations of his family, and even of his courtiers, presumably out of obsequious deference to the King. Bek himself was not slow to imitate his royal master: in a quartzite shrine stele (**29**) carved by the Master Sculptor in the early years of Akhenaten's reign, Bek stands alongside his wife, Taherit. She has been depicted in the conventional manner, but he has represented himself with the same pendulous breasts and protruding belly as the King. In the fifth year of Akhenaten's reign, when he

29. *Bek and Taherit: shrine stele, quartzite (Ägyptisches Museum, Berlin)*

changed his name from Amenhotep to Akhenaten, the naturalistic style of Amarna art was taken to extremes and, perhaps in order to emphasise the break with the past, sculpted figures of both Akhenaten and Nefertiti became grotesque almost to the point of caricature.

There are many unresolved puzzles concerning the Amarna Age, not least the cause of Akhenaten's supposed deformities, or even whether his physical shape was actually as it appears to be in depictions of the King. Several medical conditions have been proposed over the years to account for his appearance, ranging from a disorder of the pituitary gland known as Fröhlich's Syndrome or *dystrophia adiposogenitalis*, a condition that leads to obesity, absence of body hair and underdeveloped genital organs, to Marfan's Syndrome, an inherited disease of the connective tissue in which the sufferer grows extremely tall and thin. Certainly, portraits depict Akhenaten with thin legs and arms; but whether he was extremely tall we have no way of knowing. Another condition that has been suggested is Klinefelter's Syndrome, in which from birth an apparent male has breasts that are female in appearance, small testes, and disproportionately long limbs, especially the legs. He later develops a high-pitched voice and poor facial hair growth. One of the sandstone colossi of Akhenaten unearthed at Waset depicts him nude and without genitalia. However this may have been done for religious reasons in order to portray him as an hermaphrodite, to convey the message that he, like the Aten, was a god who was both father and mother. There is no need to make up elaborate theories on how a man without genitalia could father six daughters. Theories range from the unfortunate Akhenaten being stricken with Fröhlich's Syndrome, conveniently, only after the birth of his children, to the even more unfortunate Akhenaten being cuckolded by Nefertiti with a variety of surrogate fathers, my own favourite candidate for the position being General Horemheb!

Whether or not the ancient Egyptians suffered from any of these diseases we do not know; but recently, another medical disorder has been found to account for Akhenaten's appearance. This is lipodystrophy, a disturbance of fat metabolism in which the subcutaneous fat disappears over some regions of the body but is unaffected in others. In progressive lipodystrophy the loss of fat is confined to the upper part of the body above the pelvis; and the subcutaneous fat of the buttocks may be increased. General health remains unimpaired but there may be psychological disturbances. About eighty percent of cases are female; and onset of lipodystrophy occurs early in life: in fifty percent of cases before the age of ten, in seventy-five percent before the age of twenty.

Lipodystrophy would account nicely for both Akhenaten's physical appearance as represented in statues and reliefs; and any 'psychological disturbances' resulting from the disease could have led to his religious excesses. However, what if it were not Akhenaten who suffered from the condition, but Nefertiti, who developed it in her teens? If this were so, then perhaps Akhenaten had himself portrayed with the same physical deformities as his once beautiful wife whose changed appearance became his ideal of female beauty. But of course, in the absence of Akhenaten's body, or those of Nefertiti and their children, we cannot know whether they in any way resembled their 'portraits'. That being the case, arguments over Akhenaten's appearance and the possible causes of it can only be speculative and based on an over-interpretation of the data.

We know that it was a convention of ancient Egyptian art not to show human beings as they really were, 'warts and all', but to represent them in an idealised way. For the most part art had a funerary purpose in that it was a representation of things as they would be in the Afterlife. In their portrayal of Akhenaten his artists may have been trying to express a different concept of kingship and godhead by exaggerating slightly unusual aspects of the King's appearance in an elaboration of one of the aims of ancient Egyptian art, which was to show things as they are known to be rather than as they happen to look at a particular time or from a particular angle — an ideal, ironically, that artists of the twentieth-century Cubist movement shared. It may be that artistic representations of Akhenaten are as much a distortion of visual reality as the paintings of Picasso in his Cubist period: but if in the future archaeologists were to excavate the work that inspired Cubism, *Les Demoiselles d'Avignon*, would they assume that its distortion of the human form accurately portrayed women of the first decade of the twentieth century? Thus we also may be mistaken in assuming that Akhenaten in any way resembled his supposed portraits.

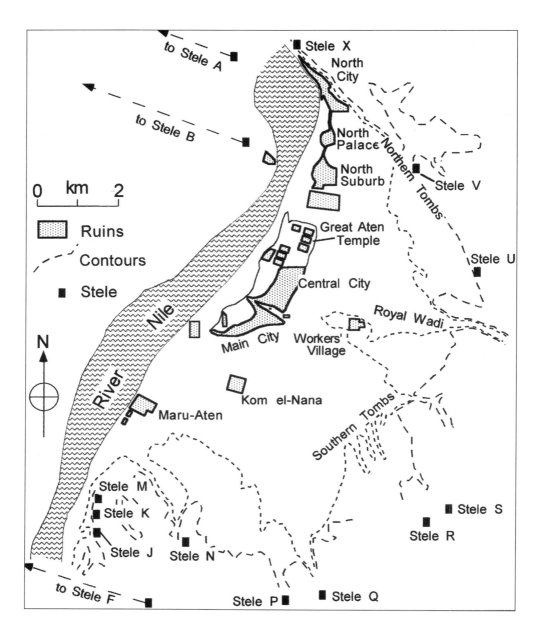

Fig. 3. Tell El-Amarna

5. Akhetaten — the Horizon of the Aten

Every major deity in ancient Egypt laid claim to a place of origin, the location in which he or she was said to have brought the world into existence. Until the reign of Akhenaten, the Aten had no such place of origin, and it was thus imperative that the King should create one for him. A virgin site on the east bank of the Nile roughly half way between Waset and Inebhedj was the location chosen — by the Aten himself, it was claimed. It has been surmised that the reason for choosing it was because of its appearance: a semicircular ridge of limestone cliffs which touch the river at the northern end of the site and again some 6 miles (10km) further south, forming a bay filled with a flat layer of sand up to three and a half miles (5km) across at its widest point. This configuration bore a marked resemblance to the hieroglyphic sign for 'horizon' — 𓈌 — that was an element in the name of the new religious centre and royal city: Akhetaten, the Horizon of the Aten.

Work had begun on building Akhetaten by the fourth year of Akhenaten's reign and proceeded apace. Within a year the city was formally dedicated to the Aten in a ceremony that was commemorated on three stelae carved into the cliffs at the northern and southern ends of the site. These stelae, which are known to Egyptologists by the letters X, M and K, are now badly damaged and the dates on them illegible but may have been Regnal Year 5. Parts of the texts remain and on each stele the King relates how he planned Akhetaten and dedicated it to the Aten. A year later, eight more stelae were cut at strategic points in the cliffs that formed the backdrop to the city to the east; and another three (**30**) across the river (**colour plate 11**) at the western edge of the wide fertile plain that stretches 12 miles (20km) across before it reaches the desert. The 14 Boundary Stelae, which marked the limits of the city and its rural hinterland, together described a rough circle so that the 'Horizon of the Aten' stretched from one sky-line to the other on both sides of the Nile. All the stelae show Akhenaten, Nefertiti and two of their daughters worshipping the Aten. The inscription[59] on each is basically the same and begins with the date and the names and epithets of the King, followed by the names and epithets of Nefertiti, who is called, typically, 'the lady of grace, the fair of face ... at the sound of whose voice One (the King) rejoices'. On the stele (S) that marks the southeastern boundary Akhenaten swears by his love for Nefertiti and her children that, 'as she be allowed to live into old age in the care of the King, and as the princesses Meretaten and Meketaten, her children, be allowed to live into old age in the care of the Queen, their mother ... the southern stele which is on the eastern mountain of Akhetaten ... I shall let stand in its place. I shall never pass southward beyond it'.

30. Boundary Stele A, Tuna el-Gebel, showing Akhenaten and Nefertiti, with princesses Meretaten and Meketaten

The inscription on the stele continues:

> The southwestern stele has been fashioned to face it on the southern mountain of Akhetaten, directly opposite. The middle stele on the eastern mountain ... I shall let stand in its place on the eastern horizon of Akhetaten. I shall never pass eastward beyond it. The middle stele on the western mountain of Akhetaten has been fashioned to face it directly opposite. The northeastern stele of Akhetaten I shall let stand in its place: it is the northern stele of Akhetaten. I shall never pass northward beyond it. The northern stele which is on the western mountain of Akhetaten has been fashioned to face it directly opposite.

Akhnaten's statements that he will 'never pass beyond' the boundaries marked by the stelae have been understood to mean that he was vowing never to leave Akhetaten. However, it is more probable that he was undertaking never to enlarge the city limits of Akhetaten, perhaps because it was conceived to be perfectly realised at the outset in conformity with the will of the Aten. Thus the city on the east bank of the Nile, a ribbon development of buildings, together with the farmland on the west bank, was allotted from the beginning an area measuring some 112 square miles (290sq.km). The urban area alone measured at least 1100 acres (440ha) and may have occupied up to 3000 acres (1200ha).

The construction of such a large city was a tremendous undertaking: but the challenge

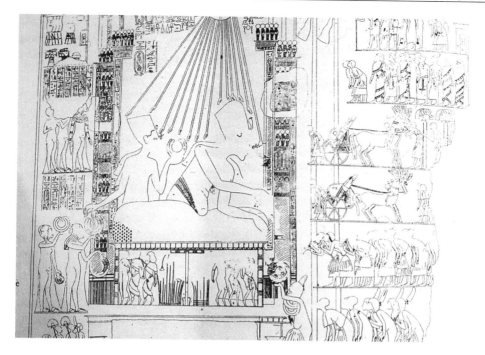

31.   *Window of Appearances. Drawing by N. Davies (see caption to text photograph 23) of a relief in the tomb of Meryre, Tell el-Amarna*

was met and in a very short period of time palaces, temples, administrative and storage buildings and workshops had been erected, together with housing to accommodate hundreds of nobles and officials and thousands of workmen, labourers and servants, together with their familes, not to mention tombs for the royal family and the nobles. Religious structures were made of stone and secular buildings were constructed from sun-dried mud-brick, as was the norm in ancient Egypt. Even the royal palaces were largely built in mud-brick, although a certain amount of stone was used — for the lintels of doors and windows, and the bases of columns, for instance — and floors were sometimes made of brick painted with scenes showing birds, plants and pools. Inevitably, there was a certain amount of jerry-building but overall standards were remarkably high.

   The first buildings to be erected at Akhetaten were the palaces and temples in an area now called the Central City, situated in the centre of the plain on the east bank of the Nile. Three major, though unpaved, roads ran from north to south through the whole city, all having streets opening off them. To the west lay the magnificent thoroughfare, some 40m wide, today known as the Sikhet es-Sultan or King's Road, which connected the palaces and temples and was the processional route from palace to temple for the royal chariot. To the east of the King's Road was a smaller road now known as Street A; and to the east of Street A was another magnificent road, in places some 50m wide. It was named by its German excavators (see p.138) the Street of the High Priests, but is known to its modern British excavators by the more mundane appellation East Road South.

The two main temples of the Aten were situated on the east side of the King's Road, with the *Per Aten* lying on the northern edge of the Central City, some 800m north of the *Ḥwt Aten*. Between the temples was the King's House, the most interesting feature of which was the so-called 'Window of Appearances' overlooking an open courtyard on its north side. The Window of Appearances (**31**) was the ancient Egyptian equivalent of the balcony at Buckingham Palace. It was the place from which Akhenaten rewarded loyal officials with necklaces made of large gold rings by throwing down the necklaces from the window to the lucky recipients assembled in the courtyard below; a presentation that every noble at Akhetaten took pains to record in his tomb. To the east of the King's House lay other buildings that made up Akhetaten's official section: police and military headquarters, and the foreign office, which housed the archives of international correspondence that in modern times have become famous as the Amarna Letters (*see* p.135 ff.).

A bridge led across the road from the King's House to a large complex of buildings on the west side. The larger part of this complex, consisting of halls and courts, was built of stone, with painted floors, and walls decorated with reliefs and adorned with brightly coloured faience inlays. Several rooms had balustrades of marbled limestone; and granite and indurated (hardened) limestone statues, twice life-sized, of the King and Queen were found within the complex. In the many-columned central hall, images of Akhenaten as a sphinx were carved on door lintels, and reliefs of Akhenaten, Nefertiti and the princesses making offerings to the Aten decorated the columns. This complex was once identified by Egyptologists as the Great Palace. However the nature of its reliefs and the use of stone in its construction would suggest that the building served a religious function, and was perhaps used first for the *heb-sed* or Jubilee that Akhenaten celebrated with the Aten, and later for grand formal receptions and religious ceremonies. In any case, the Central City was hastily built and alterations were carried out from time to time, so that what might have been first planned as a palace may later have been turned into something else.

South of the Central City lay the Main City, which was probably built soon after the official section since it contained extensive suburbs of estates belonging to courtiers and high officials, with the houses of their retainers and lesser functionaries clustered around them. The most imposing residences in this area were those of the priest, Pawah; the Master of the Horse, Renefer; the general, Ramose; the priest, Panehsy, who also had an official residence near the *Per Aten*; and the Chief Minister, Nakht. One of Nakht's titles was Overseer of Public Works, so it was he who in all probability was responsible for the erection of most of the royal and state buildings in Akhetaten. Just north of the wide *wadi* (*see* Glossary) that bisects the Main City lay a sculptors' quarter in which the studio of the master-sculptor, Thutmose (see p.139), was situated.

Nakht's mansion was typical of the type owned by the upper classes, who made up less than ten percent of the population of Akhetaten. It was 26m square, with a 9m-long vestibule at one corner, and, on the ground floor alone, 30 rooms. Almost the entire northern third of the ground floor was taken up by an eight-columned reception hall. At the centre of the building was a large hall or living room with a dais at one end, which would have been strewn with cushions for relaxing on. The central hall was equipped with a hearth against cold weather, and, surrounded as it was with smaller rooms and

32. Lavatory stool. From the house of Nakht, Tell el-Amarna (Cairo Museum)

storerooms, had a raised ceiling to allow for the insertion of clerestory windows. The interior decoration of private houses, however large, could not compare with the frescoes and painted floors of the royal palaces; but walls, especially those in the main living room, were often decorated with painted friezes and dadoes, in designs consisting mostly of stylized fruit and flowers. Nakht's mansion was no exception.

At the rear of the mansion were bedrooms and bathrooms. The master bedroom, which led from Nakht's private sitting room, had at one end a niche, formed from a thickening of the walls, in which there was a dais. Nakht's bed — a single bed for there were no double beds in ancient Egypt — stood on the dais, kept cool by the thickness of the walls around it. Its legs were placed on small stone stands; and it is possible that they stood in bowls of turpentine to prevent termites and other insects crawling up them. The *en suite* bathroom was equipped not with a bath but with the ancient Egyptian version of a shower tray, a stone slab on which the bather stood whilst a servant poured water over him. The dais had a drainage hole to allow the water to flow away into a sump; and the walls of the bathroom were lined with stone. Nakht's mansion was also equipped with earth closets with whitewashed walls; and the earliest-known lavatory stool (**32**) was recovered from one of them.

In front of the mansion was a garden, a pool; and a private chapel, open to the sky,

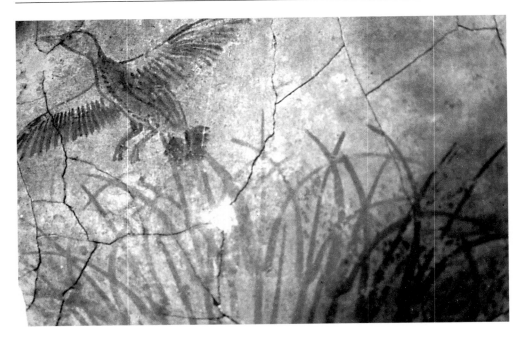

33.   Wall painting, North Palace, Tell el-Amarna (Cairo Museum)

within which was a square offering-table and, on the rear wall, a stele showing Akhenaten worshipping the Aten. Servants' quarters, kitchens, stables, byres, workshops, storerooms and offices were situated to the rear, away from the main house. As always, they lay to the east of it, a wise precaution since there is rarely an east wind in Egypt that would bring kitchen and animal smells into the master's living quarters. West of the house, in a courtyard of their own, were tall, beehive-shaped grain silos. They were arranged in pairs, with a flight of steps between each pair leading to the tops of the silos. Grain was poured into a silo from the top and extracted at the bottom by means of a small door. Nakht's mansion, like all large estates, had its own water supply in the form of a well. The whole estate was surrounded by a high wall which fronted onto the main street.

Some distance to the south of the Main City at Akhetaten was the Sunshade-temple known as the Maru-Aten (The Place from Which the Aten is Observed). It had belonged first to Kiya and then to Meretaten (*see* p.58). The Maru-Aten was a belvedere, a word defined as a structure commanding a fine view, in this case, of the Aten; and consisted of two rectangular enclosures, the northern measuring some 200m by 100, the southern some 160m by 80. The smaller enclosure boasted a pool and a pillared hall set among flowerbeds and shrubberies. In the larger enclosure over half the area was occupied by a T-shaped lake whilst the rest of the space was filled with halls, including one in which there were tanks filled with water plants, open-sided pavilions, a small temple in which there was an offering-table, and flowerbeds. Floors in the building were painted with scenes of waterfowl flying between papyrus and other water plants, and columns and walls were painted with similar scenes. Perhaps the most interesting room in the Maru-Aten was the storeroom, in the north-eastern corner of the enclosure, which was used as a wine-cellar, a detail that conjures up a vision of royal ladies relaxing in the belvedere sipping wine as they contemplated the Aten.

To the north of the Central City was a royal residence, the North Palace (**colour plate 12**), a walled, rectangular compound with courtyards and storerooms arranged around a central garden with a pool. One courtyard contained two sets of limestone mangers decorated with oxen and antelopes, suggesting that these animals were once kept there. In the north-east corner of the palace was a sunken garden surrounded by columns and small rooms with walls decorated with naturalistic scenes of birds in papyrus thickets (**33 & colour plate 17**). It was usual in ancient Egypt to decorate only the top or bottom of an interior wall, but in the Northern Palace it is clear that the entire wall surface of what is now called 'The Green Room' was painted: the bottom of each wall represent to sparkling blue water with floating lotus pads and flowers; the middle with reeds and grasses at the water's edge; and the rest of the wall with flowering shrubs and birds such as rock pigeons, palm doves, shrikes and kingfishers either nesting in the thicket or darting among the reeds in search of insects. The Northern Palace seems to have been intended for the use of female members of the royal family. Fragments of inscriptions on the walls refer only to Akhenaten's eldest daughter, Meretaten, but her name was superimposed on another, which may have been that of Nefertiti or Kiya.

Some distance to the north of the Palace, almost at the foot of the cliffs, lay the so-called North Suburb, originally planned and earmarked for a royal residence — the North Riverside Palace — surrounded by fairly large villas for the middle classes who made up about 35 percent of the population of Akhetaten. As the city grew, however, the need for more housing meant that smaller houses were crammed between the villas. Eventually old rubbish dumps were levelled to accommodate even smaller houses so that, as time went by, living conditions became more crowded, with the hovels of the building workers who were continuously employed on construction work in the city squeezed in cheek by jowl with the mansions of the rich. The size of house in the North Suburb varied greatly, depending on the social status of the owner, with the houses of the more prosperous having more rooms, but basically the houses, regardless of size, were markedly similar to each other. Typically, they were single-storey buildings of between 90 and 185m square, with the main unit of the house consisting of a portico and a square living room around which varying numbers of other rooms were grouped. This plan provided insulation from both the heat of the day and the cold at night, and necessitated the installation of clerestory windows into the tops of the living-room walls. Water was obtained either from wells shared between several houses, or from communal wells sited in public squares. The poorest houses in the North Suburb were almost identical to those constructed for the men who prepared tombs for Akhenaten and his courtiers.

The tomb-workers of Akhetaten were specialized artisans and craftsmen, brought from their village, today known as Deir el-Medina, on the west bank at Waset. At Akhetaten, they lived with their wives and families in a walled village[60] that had been specially prepared for them. It nestled in a fold in the hills close to the cliffs in which the tombs were situated, at some distance from, and out of sight of, the main city. The village, like the city itself, was policed by soldiers from two garrisons, one on the north of Akhetaten, the other on the south, who patrolled along a network of routes that can still be traced in the uninhabited desert between the city and the cliffs in which the tombs were cut, and beyond the cliffs to the east. A contingent of *Medjay*, or police, was probably billeted in the village. This did not mean, however, that the village housed a cowed and subservient workforce if the workers' village at Deir el-Medina[61] is anything to go by. Surviving documents record that at Deir el-Medina, the tomb-workers and their families lived lives full of battles over inheritance, domestic strife, love affairs and demonstrations over incompetent officials, with the occasional strike over the non-payment of wages thrown in for good measure.

At Akhetaten, the tomb-workers showed their independence by, at the most, paying lip-service to the new religion. In several village houses amulets of Hathor and Taweret have been found, as well as figures of Bes painted on walls. Hathor was the goddess of love and intoxication, the protection of women her special concern. Taweret, a hippopotamus goddess, was identified with fecundity; and Bes, represented as an ugly dwarf, was supposed to frighten away the demons who were thought to threaten women in childbirth and their new-born infants. Thus it would seem that the wives of the tomb-workers did not give up their reliance upon these old deities; and there is evidence that they and their husbands continued to worship several other gods. At the foot of the cliffs beyond the north-east corner of their village there are over 20 chapels, identified by the modern excavators[62] of the site as tomb-chapels. However, these 'tomb-chapels' have no burial shafts, nor do they display any funerary evidence. It is more likely, therefore, that they were used as shrines by the workers and their families, especially since there are benches built along the sides of the front halls. In one of the 'chapels'[63] there is a stele dedicated to Isis, wife of Osiris and the epitome of the loyal wife and caring mother, and Shed, her son, whose name means 'saviour'. This is proof that these popular deities were worshipped by the tomb-workers of Akhetaten in defiance of the theology of the king.

The workers' village was cheaply built. Although a certain amount of wood was used — for doors, for example — scarcely any stone was employed for door jambs and lintels. The houses in the village were inferior to those in the city: partition walls were only one brick thick and even the exterior walls were thin. Recent excavations at the site by the Egypt Exploration Society have revealed that the houses were built using two types of brick: one, the normal kind made of Nile mud mixed, in this instance, with gravel; and another made of the marl (limestone mud or shale) that is found in the hills around the village. It has been suggested that at the beginning, the village was supplied by the government with regular bricks, and possibly a surveyor to demonstrate how to lay out the foundations of a house; but that later on, the villagers were left to complete their houses themselves, which they did with the marl that was nearer to hand than Nile mud, and with stones. There was very little in the way of painted walls or ceilings; and, judging from excavation finds, pottery was utilitarian. The village had no wells, so that water had to be brought from the Nile, about two miles (3km) away. However, it is probable that the tomb-workers of Akhetaten lived in houses that were typical of those of contemporary artisans; and significantly better than those of the peasants.

There were about 80 houses in the workers' village, all alike in layout and size, with the exception of one larger than the rest that is presumed to have belonged to the overseer.

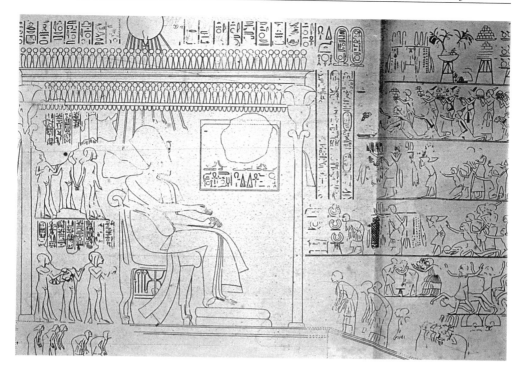

34.   *'Durbar' held in Year 12. Akhenaten and Nefertiti sit enthroned, holding hands. Behind them are their daughters: in the top row, on the right, is Meritaten; behind her is Meketaten, who is turning to smell a mandrake fruit (lost) held by Ankhesenpaaten. The three princesses wear their hair long, a sign that they have reached puberty. In the bottom row stand, from right to left, Neferneferuaten and Neferneferure, holding baby gazelles, and Setepenre, who is tickling a gazelle with her finger. Drawing by N. Davies (see caption to text photograph 23) of a relief in the tomb of Meryre, Tell el-Amarna*

Each house was some 5m wide and 10m long, divided into four sections: an entrance hall, which led to the living-room, behind which was a small bedroom and an even smaller kitchen. The door to the house was wooden and swung on a pivot; and when closed it could be secured on the inside by a wooden bar fixed between sockets on either door jamb. It had a latch worked from the outside by a cord. The roof of the house was flat with a loggia of wood and matting. The builder seems to have overlooked the need for stairs, for no space was left for them on the outside of the house where the staircase would normally have been placed. Instead, they were crammed into the entrance hall, taking up half its area; or into the kitchen, leaving no room in it for kitchen activities, which had perforce to be carried out behind a screen in the entrance hall. Entrance halls were much used. They were the places where women wove cloth on looms, and a corner of the floor might be smoothed off so that it could be used for picking over grain or kneading dough for bread- and beer-making. In another corner there was likely to be a trough for water, and a tethering-stone might be let into the floor, for at night, the family donkey, and possibly other domestic animals, were brought into the hall.

Courtiers who served Akhenaten in his new city were rewarded with lavish gifts, and with tombs cut into the faces of the cliffs that border the desert edge to the east of Akhetaten. The situation of the tombs symbolically removed them from the aegis of the God of the West (Osiris) who, as the beneficent ruler of the Underworld, was one of the most popular deities in Egypt. The decoration of the tombs, which in most cases sadly was never finished, is the art of the period at its finest. In plan the tomb-chapels resemble those constructed at Waset for the courtiers of other Eighteenth-Dynasty kings. They are rock-cut, and have either a long corridor leading to a transverse hall with a large niche on the rear wall containing a statue of the deceased; or they have a forecourt leading to a large columned hall beyond which there is a transverse hall with a statue-niche, again on the rear wall. The position of the grave shaft varies but is most often in the floor of the hall. Six of the tombs are situated in the cliffs north of the entrance to the so-called Royal *Wadi* (*see* p.91), and a further 19 lie 3 miles (5km) away to the south.

The two northernmost tombs belonged to Huya, Steward of Queen Tiye, and to Meryre, Superintendent of the Household of Queen Nefertiti. Both tombs, which were the last to be prepared, are decorated with reliefs showing Akhenaten and Nefertiti in the Hall of Foreign Tribute (**34**) receiving homage from foreign lands (*see* p.53). The scene in Meryre's tomb is one of the few places in which all six daughters of the royal couple were depicted. The tomb of Meryre, which is unfinished, is chiefly remarkable for a scene of Akhenaten, accompanied by Nefertiti, standing at the Window of Appearances to reward Meryre; and a sketch in black paint showing Meryre being rewarded by Smenkhkare (*see* p.105), Akhenaten's successor, who is accompanied by his wife, Akhenaten's eldest daughter, Meretaten. Meryre was appointed Superintendent of her household after the death of her mother. The walls of Huya's statue-niche are decorated with scenes depicting a funeral, the only such scenes at Akhetaten. It is possible that Akhenaten had not forbidden the depiction, or even the enaction, of a traditional funeral, and that it is mere chance that no funeral scenes appear in the other tombs. On the other hand it is possible that Huya, as an official of Queen Tiye, was less affected by new customs than other courtiers.

In the front hall of Huya's tomb there are three scenes depicting events during Queen Tiye's famous visit to Akhetaten in Akhenaten's 12th regnal year. They are of the presentation of her Sunshade-temple, and the banquet held in her honour at which some members of the royal family, although not Tiye, are shown eating with gusto (**35**). In one scene, Nefertiti seems to be in the act of devouring a whole roast duck whilst Akhenaten gnaws at a large bone wrapped round with strips of meat. Tiye's young daughter, Beketaten, is shown receiving a titbit from her mother. Princess Meretaten, sitting at her mother's feet with an unnamed sister, is also eating roast duck. In another scene, Akhenaten quaffs a large goblet of wine.

On the lintel above the door into the transverse hall is a scene showing Queen Tiye and Beketaten saluting Amenhotep III on one side, and on the other Akhenaten and Nefertiti being saluted by their daughters, a reminder that Huya was a devoted servant to both generations of the royal family. In another scene, Huya is rewarded for his loyalty to Akhenaten, who is shown at the Window of Appearances showering Huya with gifts of

35.   *Banquet. Drawing by N. Davies (see caption to text photograph 23) of a relief in the tomb of Huya, Tell el-Amarna*

gold necklaces and bracelets. Beneath this scene is one of a sculptor's studio in which Huya is shown 'appointing the craftsmen', one of his tasks as a high ranking administrator although he was not himself an artist. In this scene (**36**), Iuty, Master Sculptor to the Queen-in-Chief, Tiye, is depicted sitting on a stool making corrections with pen and ink to a statue of Princess Beketaten whilst the man who carved the statue stands before him, bowing deferentially. Admiring apprentices exclaim, 'How lifelike it is!'

The third of the northern group of tombs belonged to Ahmose, Fan Bearer on the Right of the King. The decoration was never finished, but on one wall Akhenaten and Nefertiti, escorted by their armed guard, are depicted driving in a chariot from the palace to the Temple of the Aten. The Queen is shown kissing the King, while a young princess leans over the front of her chariot to pat the horse. To the south of Ahmose's tomb is that of another Meryre, who was High Priest of the Aten. His tomb has in it scenes showing the Royal Palace, the harbour of Akhetaten, the state cattle barns and the ubiquitous scene of the King at the Window of Appearances. However in this case the scene is enlivened by the fact that Meryre is shown being lifted on the shoulders of his friends to receive his rewards. There are also two representations of the Temple of the Aten. In one of these Akhenaten and Nefertiti, accompanied by two of their daughters, are shown making offerings to the Aten, beneath whose disk is a unique depiction of a rainbow. The other scene shows the Royal Family entering the temple to the accompaniment of music played by blind harpists and singers.

The fifth of the northern group of tombs, that of Pentu, Chief Physician to the King, contains another representation of the Aten Temple but little else. The southernmost

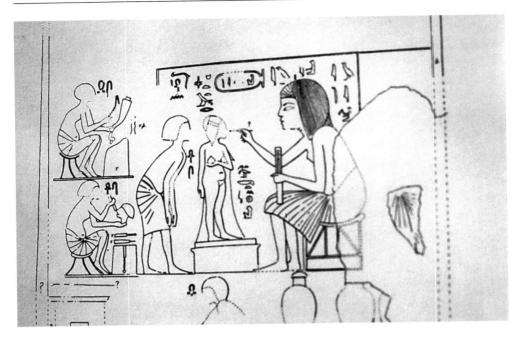

36. *Sculptor Iuty. Drawing by N. Davies (see caption to text photograph 23) of a relief in the tomb of Huya, Tell el-Amarna*

tomb in this group belonged to Panehsy (*see* p.82), Chief Servitor of the Aten, Superintendent of the Cattle of the Aten, Superintendent of the Granary of the Aten, and Chancellor of Lower Egypt. Unusually, there is a relief in the tomb depicting Panehsy as an obese, elderly man, accompanied by his daughter, adoring the Aten. Otherwise, the tomb is decorated with the usual scenes of the royal family in their chariots making their way to the Aten temple or adoring the Aten, including one on the right of the entrance which shows Nefertiti's sister, Mutnodjmet (*see* p.130), with two dwarves in attendance. Some 1600 years after Akhetaten was built, Egypt had converted to Christianity, and Coptic (native Egyptian) hermits re-occupied ancient tombs throughout Middle Egypt. A large community grew up around the northern group of tombs at what once had been Akhetaten, and their huts, built of rough, dry-stone walls, are still to be seen clinging to the hillside. The tomb of Panehsy was partly enlarged and became their church.

The northernmost tomb of the southern group belonged to Parennefer, Washer of the King's Hands and Chief Craftsman, the son of Apuia, who had been the Chief Craftsman of Amenhotep III. His tomb is chiefly remarkable for a scene depicting Parennefer receiving rewards from Akhenaten, which is more than usually lively. The second tomb in the group belonged to the Chamberlain, Tutu (*see* p.60). Tutu's tomb, though unfinished, was clearly intended to be one of the most elaborate at Akhetaten, and boasts a particularly magnificent hall with 12 columns arranged in two rows. Its decoration includes a scene of Tutu being lavishly rewarded by the King and driving home in his chariot to much acclaimation from the throng which, perhaps significantly, includes Asiatics.

The third tomb in the southern group belonged to Mahu, Chief of the Medjay (police) and contains a number of lively scenes depicting episodes in Mahu's career. In one the King inspects a row of guard boxes, with Mahu in attendance; in another Mahu draws supplies for his men; and in a third Mahu triumphantly captures three foreign criminals. The liveliest scene shows the royal chariot leaving the temple with the Chief Minister, as was the custom, running alongside it. In this instance, the Chief Minister is old and fat, and is cruelly depicted struggling to keep up. The next four tombs belong to Ipy, the Royal Scribe; Ramose, Steward of the House of Nebmaatre (Amenhotep III); Nakht, Chief Minister and Chancellor (*see* p.82); and Neferkheperuhersekheper, Governor of Akhetaten.

The eighth tomb in the southern group belonged to Maya, Fan Bearer on the Right of the King, Royal Chancellor and Supervisor of the Soldiery. This tomb, like that of Tutu, was intended to have a 12-columned hall, and in it is another representation of Mutnodjmet (*see* above), again accompanied by her two dwarves. Maya seems to have fallen out of favour before he died, for his name was erased and his figure plastered over. The tombs south of Maya's belonged to Suti, Standard-bearer of the Guild of Neferkheperure (Akhenaten), followed by three uninscribed tombs. The 13th tomb in the southern group belonged to Setau, Overseer of the Treasury; the next three are uninscribed.

The 17th tomb in the southern group belonged to Any, Scribe of the Altar and the Offering Table of the Aten. Amazingly, an inscription in the tomb describes Any as having been the Steward of the Household of Aakheperure (Amenhotep II), a king who had been dead for over 45 years. Any must therefore have been a very old man; and is depicted as such in his tomb, where reliefs show him with the sunken cheeks of the toothless. The tomb to the south of Any's belonged to Paatenemheb, Commander of the Troops and Overseer of Porters.

The tomb next to Paatenemheb's, the southernmost of the tombs, belonged to the Divine Father, Ay, Fan Bearer on the Right of the King and Master of the Horse. It was clearly meant to be the most imposing of all but was never finished: although in the left half of its hall are 12 columns, grouped into three rows of four columns each, only three columns were completed in the right half of the hall. Only one scene was carved. It shows Ay and his wife, Tey, being rewarded by the royal family with gifts of golden necklaces and vases, and with a fine pair of red gloves for Ay, and is the only known instance of a woman being honoured in this way. Ay, who was probably Amenhotep III's brother-in-law, may also have been Nefertiti's father (*see* p.48). He was certainly Akhenaten's valued counsellor, and was a powerful member of the court, meriting an imposing burial place. However his tomb at Akhetaten was never used, for Ay became King of Egypt (*see* p.129) and thus merited an even more imposing place of interment.

Akhenaten chose a site for his own tomb just over four miles (7km) up the steep-sided *wadi* that bisects the cliffs containing the tombs of his courtiers. It was cut into the bedrock on the north (left-hand) side of the *wadi*, and in its basic plan is similar to the royal tombs of the Eighteenth Dynasty at Waset. A flight of 20 steps with a ramp in the centre leads into a long, gently sloping passage, at the bottom of which is a steep stairway. The passage, or entrance corridor (which is undecorated), is large, measuring some 3.5m wide by 3.5m high by nearly 23m long. A series of small rooms and corridors leads off the middle of the east (right-hand) wall of the entrance corridor, an arrangement that is unique to this tomb. This part of the tomb may have been intended for the burial of members of the Royal Family, possibly even of Nefertiti, but it was scarcely begun. The diorite and dolerite pounders with which the walls would have been smoothed were still lying abandoned in it when French excavators examined the tomb just over a hundred years ago.

At the top of the stairway, to the east, is the suite of three tomb chambers belonging to Princess Meketaten, the first room of which contains the famous relief, now badly damaged, of Akhenaten and Nefertiti mourning Meketaten (*see* p.57). At the bottom of the stairway is a sump, designed to catch any floodwater that might cascade into the lowest part of the tomb. Beyond it is the burial chamber, a spacious hall with two pillars in its western half, and a raised plinth for the sarcophagus in the centre of the space between the pillars and the eastern wall. The sarcophagus, made of red granite, was smashed to pieces by Akhenaten's opponents after his death.[64] At each of its four corners was a female figure carved in high relief, her arms outstretched in protection. Normally such figures represented the goddesses Isis, Nephthys, Neit and Selkis, but inscriptions on the sarcophagus identify the figures on Akhenaten's sarcophagus as Nefertiti (**colour plate 13**). Thus Akhenaten, having denied the existence to the old protective deities, chose to place himself under the eternal protection of his beloved wife.

Walls and pillars in the burial chamber were originally decorated with reliefs showing the Royal Family worshipping the Aten; but, probably shortly after Akhenaten's death, one of the pillars was reduced to rubble and the reliefs hacked at and badly damaged. H.W. Fairman, a member of the expedition that re-excavated the Royal Tomb in 1932, was able to discern the name of Nefertiti in many of the damaged inscriptions — in so many, in fact, that he began to wonder if the burial chamber had been intended for Nefertiti. Certainly, local villagers digging illicitly in the Royal *Wadi* in 1881 found a hoard of jewellery that had been secreted in or near the tomb, in which there was a gold ring that had belonged to her.

In the area around the Royal Tomb are the unfinished cuttings of other tombs, and it is possible that Akhenaten intended to begin a new 'Valley of the Tombs of the Kings' in which he and his successors would be buried. However, nothing is known of the circumstances surrounding the end of his reign; the manner and whereabouts of his death and burial remain mysteries, as do those of Nefertiti and most other members of the Royal Family. In 1891–92, officials from the Egyptian Antiquities Service found a mummy outside the Royal Tomb. Its bandages had been ripped away in the attempt to retrieve the gold protective amulets that tomb-robbers knew to be scattered between the wrappings. The body within had been torn to shreds, but the rumour grew that this was all that remained of Akhenaten. It is much more probable, however, that his followers had removed his body to a place of safety once the backlash against the Atenist era had begun. Sadly, Akhenaten's promise on the earlier boundary stelae at Akhetaten that he, Nefertiti and Meretaten would be buried at Akhetaten, and that if any of them were to die elsewhere, their bodies should be brought back to the Horizon of the Aten for burial, was probably not realised. It is very likely that when Akhetaten was abandoned, all the bodies in the Royal Tomb were removed to Waset for re-burial.

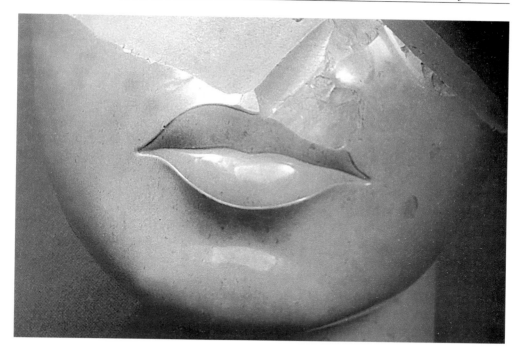

37.   Fragment of an Amarna queen's head, yellow jasper (Metropolitan Museum, New York)

The great English Egyptologist, W.M. Flinders Petrie (1853–1942), who began work at the site of Akhetaten in 1891, was the first person to note that in its tombs a new style of art had been introduced. It is Akhenaten who has been given the credit for 'inventing' what is today called the Amarna style, although an incipient Amarna style can be seen in the art of his father's reign. Whether or not this genuinely distinctive style was simply a natural development of traditional Egyptian art, it is nevertheless an extremely attractive, sometimes exquisite, genre (**37, 38, 39 and colour plate 14**). At first glance, it seems to be original in its realism and naturalness. However, all the old Egyptian principles and conventions of art are still there, especially in the canon of proportion employed in the drawing of the human figure, and in the convention that the most important person in any group should be depicted larger in scale than the others. A talent for representing the natural world was not special to the Amarna style, as can be seen in private tombs from the Fourth Dynasty onwards.

The main departure from convention was in the depiction of the figure of the King, which was shown with all its apparent deformities, which were often reproduced in depictions of his family and his courtiers. In conventional Egyptian art, kings, their families and those among their subjects privileged enough to own tombs decorated with scenes showing them engaged in the activities of their daily lives, and the statues that were placed within the tombs, were portrayed in an idealised manner and not as they might be in real life. Kings were living gods, and, unlike Akhenaten, Nefertiti and their daughters, were never portrayed in intimate scenes kissing wives and children (**40**).

38.   *Torso of an unidentified Amarna queen or princess, red quartzite (Musée du Louvre, Paris)*

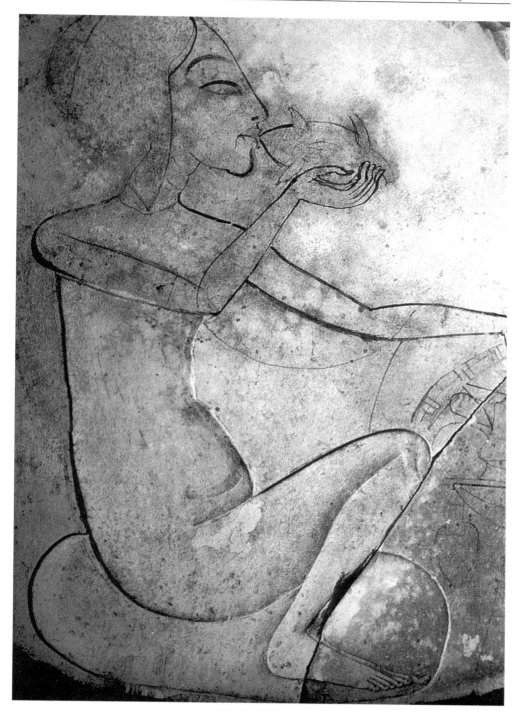

39.   *Princess eating duck: sculptor's trial piece, limestone (Cairo Museum)*

40. *Akhenaten kissing princess Meretaten: detail of limestone shrine stele (Ägyptisches Museum, Berlin)*

41. *Nefertiti, with princess Meketaten on her knee and princess Ankhesenpaaten on her shoulder:*
     detail of limestone shrine stele (Ägyptisches Museum, Berlin)

42. *Akhenaten giving an earring to princess Meretaten, whilst princess Meketaten tickles her mother under her chin: limestone shrine stele (Cairo Museum)*

The Amarna style, however, was marked by its depictions of the unselfconscious fondness shown to each other by members of the royal family (**41 & 42**). The Amarna style may be 'realistic', at least in the case of Akhenaten himself, or 'naturalistic'; equally, it may be said to be just a different convention.

It is fitting that of the very few ancient Egyptian artists whose names are known to us, four made contributions to the Amarna style. The first is Men, Amenhotep III's Master Sculptor, who must have been influential in developing the style of his son, Bek (*see* p.74), who became Akhenaten's Master Sculptor. Iuty, Master Sculptor to Queen Tiye, is also known, as is Thutmose, who was not only a sculptor but also Chief of Works and therefore responsible for supervising other sculptors as well as building projects.

43. *Nefertiti: head from workshop of the sculptor, Thutmose, Tell el-Amarna, yellow quartzite (Ägyptisches Museum, Berlin)*

Thutmose was an artist whose style can be recognized. Outstanding amongst his works[65] are the painted limestone bust of Nefertiti that is perhaps the most famous depiction of the Queen (**colour plate 9**); an unfinished yellow quartzite head of Nefertiti which, like the limestone bust, depicts her as a young woman whose lips are upturned at the corners in a slight smile (**43**); and an exquisite limestone statuette which depicts her as an older woman, with two deep lines at the sides of her mouth and the flesh of her cheeks sagging (**44**).

Three quartzite heads of princesses, about two-thirds life-size, were found in Thutmose's workshop (**45 & colour plate 15**). They are chiefly remarkable for their exaggeratedly elongated shaven skulls (**46**) which some have suggested was due to an illness such as hydrocephalus and others to the binding of the heads in infancy in order to produce an elongated effect. As so often with the Amarna Age this is speculation based on an absence of data: none of the princesses' bodies have survived so that medical examination is not possible; and there is no convincing explanation for such a deliberate malformation of the skull. The

44. *Nefertiti: head of statuette from workshop of the sculptor, Thutmose, Tell el-Amarna, limestone (Ägyptisches Museum, Berlin)*

45.   *Head of an unidentified Amarna princess from workshop of the sculptor, Thutmose, Tell el-Amarna, red quartzite (Cairo Museum)*

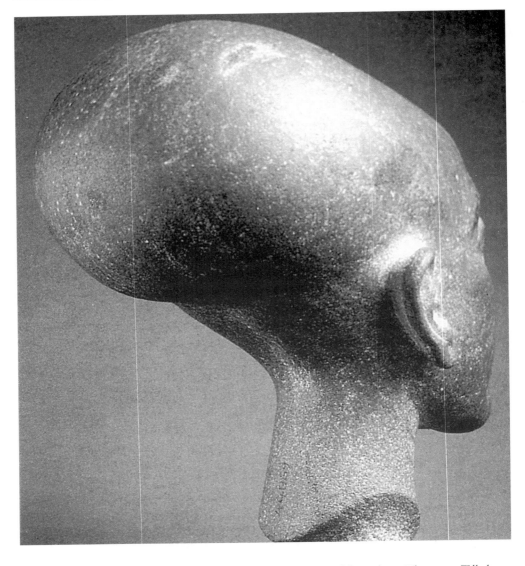

46. *Head of an unidentified Amarna princess from workshop of the sculptor, Thutmose, Tell el-
     Amarna, red quartzite (Cairo Museum)*

simplest explanation is also the most reasonable: the heads are not portraits but have a
symbolic meaning, for, viewed from the back, each skull has been carved in the shape of an
egg. Thus the skulls link the princesses with creation, which according to some ancient
Egyptian theologies came about when a divine bird hatched from an egg. Also found in
Thutmose's workshop were 23 heads made of gypsum plaster depicting royal and non-royal
people (**47 & 48**). Petrie thought that such heads were death masks, but it is now realised that
they were casts taken from work in progress to show to the supervising sculptor for correcting
or modifying.

47. *Akhenaten (?):*
    plaster cast from
    workshop of the
    sculptor,
    Thutmose, Tell el-
    Amarna
    (Ägyptisches
    Museum, Berlin)

At the height of its occupation, Akhetaten must have housed several tens of thousands of people, but its splendour and importance were short-lived. After Akhenaten died, he was succeeded first by Smenkhkare (*see* Chapter 6) and then by Tutankhaten (*see* Chapter 7), still a young boy, who soon abandoned Akhetaten for the traditional residences at Inebhedj and Waset. Amen-Re was reinstated as the chief god of Egypt and, at the same time, the worship of the Aten probably came to an end. Sometime later, possibly under Horemheb (*see* Chapter 7), or perhaps under the Nineteenth-Dynasty King, Sety I (1294–1279BC), a wave of destructive rage was unleashed against Akhenaten and his monuments. Temples and palaces bearing his name were demolished and his inscriptions and statues defaced or smashed into small pieces. His name became anathema and he was referred to as 'that criminal of Akhetaten'. Large quantities of stone blocks were removed from the city, and many were taken across the Nile to be re-used in structures built in the reigns of Ramesses II (1279–1213BC) and Sety II (1200–1194BC) at Khemenu, capital of the Hare District within the boundaries of which Akhetaten lay. Akhetaten became a city abandoned by all bar the squatters living in its empty ruins.

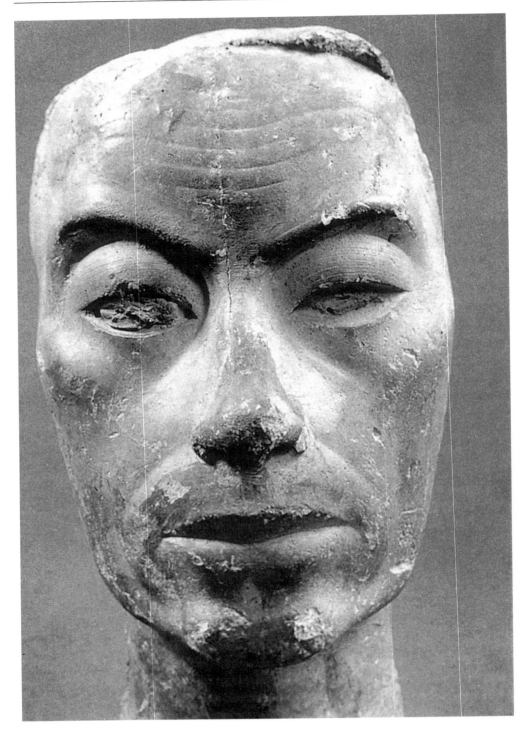

48. *Ay (?): plaster cast from workshop of the sculptor, Thutmose, Tell el-Amarna (Ägyptisches Museum, Berlin)*

6. Smenkhkare and the mystery of Tomb 55

A year or so before he died, Akhenaten seems to have appointed a young man named Smenkhkare (The Spirit of Re is Ennobled) as his co-ruler, giving his eldest daughter, Meretaten, to him as wife. Evidence that Smenkhkare married Meretaten comes from the tomb of Meryre (*see* p.88), in which an elaborate relief depicts Akhenaten, accompanied by Nefertiti, rewarding Meryre; and a sketch in the unfinished, and therefore later, part of the tomb, shows a king and queen, identified by their *cartouches* as Smenkhkare and Meretaten, performing the same act. It seems probable, therefore, that Akhenaten, who had himself married Meretaten, elected to replace her as his Queen-in-Chief with her sister, Ankhesenpaaten, so that Meretaten could be passed on to Smenkhkare in order to strengthen his claim to the throne (**colour plate 16**). A *graffito* in the tomb of Pere[66] at Waset refers to Regnal Year 3 of King Ankhkheperure Smenkhkare, and also mentions that his memorial temple was being built in the domain of Amun. From this it is reasonable to infer that Smenkhkare was intending to be buried at Waset in the traditional way. Meretaten probably died shortly after her father, at which point Smenkhkare may have married Ankhesenpaaten.[67]

Even before Akhenaten died, Atenism was a spent force, and Ankhkheperure (Living are the Manifestations of Re) Smenkhkare (1338–1336BC) made no attempt to perpetuate a cult that held no appeal for ordinary Egyptians. They preferred the comfort of their own local gods and, particularly, of Osiris, who for centuries had offered them the hope of a better life to come. Akhenaten had swept away from the official state religion Osiris and the other deities, and put nothing in their place. It is not surprising, therefore, that it was only at Akhetaten that the worship of the Aten was undertaken with any enthusiasm. Smenkhkare abandoned Akhetaten in favour of Waset, and made his peace with the old religion and with Amun in particular. Scarcely had he done so than he was dead. His successor, Tutankhaten, signified his return to the old religion by replacing the 'Aten' element in his name so that he became Tutankhamun (Living Image of Amun).

With Smenkhkare and Tutankhamun there arises yet another of the puzzles that abound in this period of Egyptian history: who were they? As Akhenaten's successors, they must have been members of the royal family; but what relationship did they bear to the King? The possibility of Akhenaten having had sons exercised the minds of Egyptologists for many years. The evidence showed that he had six daughters; and the pride that their father took in them seemed apparent from the number of times he appeared with them and their

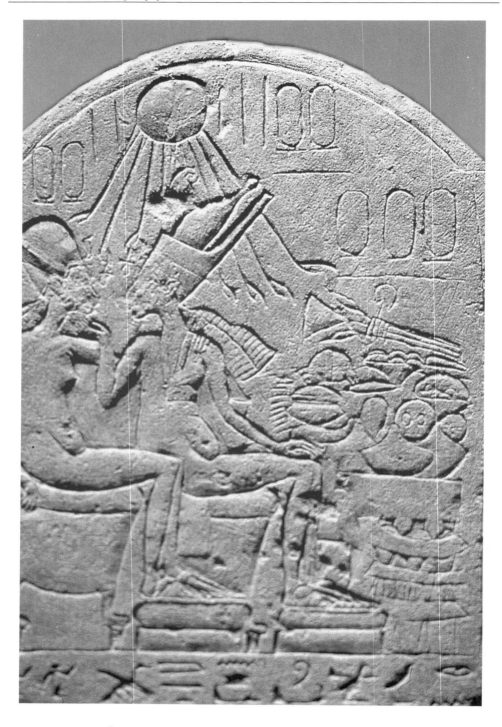

49.   *Stele of Pasi (Ägyptisches Museum, Berlin)*

mother, Nefertiti, in reliefs. Surely, the argument went, if Akhenaten had had a son then he would have recorded the fact with equal pride: but no such record had come to light. It seemed unlikely, therefore, that either Smenkhkare or Tutankhamun could have been a son of Akhenaten. Objects inscribed with the name of Tutankhaten were found at Akhetaten, indicating that as a child he lived there; but of Smenkhkare there was no sign until, as an adult, he appeared in the sketch in the tomb of Meryre.

It is a fact that, throughout the Eighteenth Dynasty, there is an absence of princes' names from royal monuments, for in this period most royal sons played a token part in the administration of Egypt, and even then only during the reigns of their fathers, and were thus denied opportunities to make their marks as individuals. It would have been rare, therefore, for the name of a son of Akhenaten to appear in the official records. Daughters were kept in obscurity and the prominence of the princesses at Akhetaten was unusual. However, the name of Tutankhaten was found in an inscription on a block of stone that had been reused at Khemenu but probably originated from the wall of a temple in Akhetaten. The inscription reads 'the son of the King, of his own body, his beloved Tutankhaten' and is taken by many to be evidence that Akhenaten was the father of Tutankhaten — but not by Nefertiti. Today, the favourite candidate for the mother of this particular prince is Queen Kiya.

The fact that Smenkhkare's name has no 'Aten' element in it would seem to indicate that he was not given his name during the Aten period. Smenkhkare, therefore, is possibly a younger son of Amenhotep III and Tiye. If this is the case then the puzzle is why was Akhenaten directly succeeded by his brother rather than by his son? The answer to this, perhaps, is that Tutankhaten was an infant at the critical time and the country needed an adult as king. The relief on a limestone votive stele (**49**) dedicated by a soldier named Pasi was seized upon by some early Egyptologists as evidence for the position Smenkhkare held in the affections of Akhenaten. The relief shows two kings, neither identified by their *cartouches*, which are empty, but one unmistakably Akhenaten, turning round to chuck the other under the chin. This king, supposed to be Smenkhkare, wears the Khepresh or Blue Crown, a sort of leather crash helmet worn whilst driving a war chariot. One interpretation of the scene was that Smenkhkare was assuming the iconographic role that Nefertiti had once fulfilled, but others reluctantly put forward the relief as evidence of a shocking intimacy between the two men. However, there is no need for such an assumption: the figure could reasonably be Nefertiti herself, wearing the Blue Crown because, as we have seen (p.52), she was not incapable of playing a warlike role.

The mystery of Smenkhkare's relationship to the royal family of Akhetaten may one day be solved thanks to one small tomb and its contents, although when Egyptologists first discovered the tomb the name of Smenkhkare was not immediately associated with it. The tomb, today known as KV55 or Tomb 55, is in the Valley of the Kings, and lies just a few metres to the west of KV6, which belonged to the Twentieth-Dynasty king, Ramesses IX (1126–1108BC). Its blocked entrance, plaster still intact and stamped with the jackal-and-nine-captives seal of the necropolis priests, was uncovered on 6 January 1907 by Edward R. Ayrton (1882–1914), a young English Egyptologist who had been appointed a year previously as chief excavator to Theodore M. Davis (1837–1915). Davis was an American lawyer and millionaire who became interested in Egyptology on his first visit to Egypt in

50.   *Tomb 55, Valley of the Kings: excavators: right to left, E.R. Ayrton and T.M. Davis, with antiquities inspector A. Weigall and his wife, Hortense*

1899. Between 1903 and 1912 he held a permit to explore the Valley of the Kings under the supervision of the Egyptian Antiquities Service, and in 1905 his then chief excavator, James Quibell, discovered the tomb of Yuya and Thuya — an event that more than encouraged Davis to continue excavating (**50**).

On the morning of 9 January 1907, the remains of the original entrance to Tomb 55 were removed. Ayrton, Davis and the American artist, Joseph Lindon Smith (1863–1950), accompanied by Arthur Weigall as the representative of the Antiquities Service, entered a sloping corridor, some 10m long. It was partly filled with limestone chippings that spilled over into the room beyond — the tomb's only chamber, which measured a little under 5 x 6m. On top of the chippings in the corridor was a large side-panel and a door-leaf, and further into the tomb the excavators found more pieces — a second door-leaf, the roof, the left side- and end-panels — of what proved to be the dismantled parts of a large shrine made of cedarwood overlaid with gold leaf. The side panels of the shrine, which was of the type that housed a coffin during burial ceremonies, were badly damaged, but on the end panel (**51 & 52**) was the figure of a queen, identified by her *cartouches* as Tiye, worshipping the Aten. In front of her stood her son, Akhenaten; but here, as everywhere on the shrine, his figure and *cartouches* had been chiselled out.

In the right-hand wall of the tomb-chamber was a niche in which there were four

51.   *Tomb 55, Valley of the Kings: shrine: panel showing Tiye standing behind Akhenaten, whose figure has been chiselled out [from T.M. Davis, The Tomb of Queen Tĩyi, 1910]*

52.   Tomb 55: shrine: line drawing of text photograph 51

calcite canopic jars (**53 & 54**) (*see* Glossary) with portrait-head stoppers (**55, 56, 57 & 58**). Below the niche, on the floor of the chamber, was an anthropoid coffin (*see* below), or mummy-case, standing on a lion-headed bier made of gilded wood. Four mud bricks, placed in the tomb for magical purposes, were scattered to the four cardinal points. The inscriptions on the bricks were largely illegible but on two the name of Akhenaten could be discerned. Amongst the debris on the floor of the chamber were the remains of wooden boxes and fragments of furniture. There were also models of, amongst other things, knives and throwing-sticks, papyrus-rolls and grapes, two statuettes of the god Bes, and small clay sealings[68] impressed with the names of Amenhotep III and Tutankhamun. The names of Amenhotep III, Tiye and Sitamun were found on funerary objects of faience and stone that had been spilled out of collapsed wooden boxes.

The wooden coffin,[69] which is of the *rishi* type (*see* Glossary), is 1.75 m long and 0.56 m wide, and was considered by the excavators to be the most highly decorated that had been discovered (**59**). On other *rishi* coffins, the feathers had simply been engraved on a thin coating of plaster, which was then gilded. However on this coffin the feathers are multi-coloured and made up of cavities cut into the wood and inlaid with stone — carnelian for the red, crystal or crystallized gypsum for the white — and glass, coloured with metallic salts to produce turquoise and lapis blue, and emerald green (**colour plate 18**). The lid of the coffin is in the shape of a human body lying stretched out, wrapped in a feather-patterned shawl. From the shawl emerge the hands, crossed over the breast, and the head, which is represented wearing an elaborate wig made of pieces of ebony inserted into the wood of the coffin.

53.   *Tomb 55: canopic jars [from Davis, 1910]*

54.   *Tomb 55: canopic jars [from Davis, 1910]*

55.   *Tomb 55: canopic jar stopper [from Davis, 1910]*

56.   Tomb 55: canopic jar stopper [from Davis, 1910]

57.   *Tomb 55: canopic jar stopper [from Davis, 1910]*

58.   *Tomb 55: canopic jar stopper [from Davis, 1910]*

59. Tomb 55: coffin [from Davis, 1910]

The sheet-gold that once overlaid the face has been ripped off, leaving only the forehead and one eyelid still covered (**60**). Although the face has a feminine cast, a false beard of the kind that linked a king with Osiris has been appended to the chin. Bands of gold running down the length of the mummy-case from arms to feet, on both the exterior and the interior of the lid, are inscribed with the titles of a king, as is the foot of the case. However the *cartouches* which would have identitified the owner have been carefully excised.

On 25 January 1907, the lid of the mummy-case was lifted. Beneath it lay the base standing on the lion-headed bier, both rotted away by damp and lying in a shallow pool of water that had probably seeped through a crack in the ceiling of the tomb over the centuries. The mummy inside the case was also badly rotted, and the excavators, accompanied by Gaston Maspero (*see* p. 138), watched whilst Joseph Lindon Smith, according to his own account,[70] attempted to examine it. The decayed wrappings which, Maspero observed, were scanty and although fine in texture very worn, were removed to reveal the body, its left arm crossed over its chest, its right extended, each adorned with three gold bracelets. The head, which had evidently been broken away from the body by an ancient rock-fall, was wrapped in a vulture pectoral of thin sheet gold. As Smith rummaged through the bandages over the chest trying to retrieve the beads of a many-stranded necklace, the wrappings disintegrated, and the flesh of the mummy 'crumbled into ashes and sifted down through the bones'.

60.   *Tomb 55: head of coffin (Cairo Museum)*

The human remains in Tomb 55 were thus reduced to a skull with a broken face, and a skeleton. In his account of the finding of the tomb, Theodore Davis reported that he had had the skeleton examined by 'two surgeons who happened to be in the Valley of the Kings'.[71] On such an unscientific basis was the width of the pelvis pronounced to be consonant with it being that of a woman; and this 'evidence' together with the name on the shrine convinced a delighted Davis that he had found both the tomb and the body of Queen Tiye. A few months later, the Australian anthropologist, G. Elliot Smith (1871–1937), at that time Professor of Anatomy in the Cairo School of Medicine, examined the remains and concluded that they were those of a young man who, 'judged by the ordinary European standards of ossification, must have attained the age of about 25 or 26 years at the time of his death.'[72] Davis had to accept that he had not found the body of his 'great queen', but as far as he was concerned the tomb belonged to her; and when the excavation report was published in 1910, he entitled it *The Tomb of Queen Tîyi*.

Tomb 55 and its contents have become one of Egyptology's most controversial discoveries, exciting much argument[73] over the ownership of the tomb and the identity of the body that was found within it. That much of the funerary furniture had originally been intended for persons other than the man buried in the tomb is undoubted: the shrine had been made for Queen Tiye, and the canopic jars had originally been made for Queen Kiya. The inscriptions on the jars were erased, and it has been claimed that the portrait-head stoppers are so ill-fitting[74] that they must have been made for a different set of jars. In that case they possibly represent not Kiya but Smenkhkare and Meretaten. The Russian Egyptologist, I.I. Perepelkin, claims that the phraseology of the text in the inscriptions on the *rishi* coffin formed part of a titulary unique to Kiya.[75] This would suggest that although the coffin had originally been intended for Kiya, for some reason she was not buried in it, and the inscriptions were altered to take the name of a king, at which time the seemingly incongruous false beard was added to the face. Thus it is clear that a considerable amount of recycling had gone on in order to equip Tomb 55.

It is reasonable to assume that at the end of the Atenist period Tiye's body would have been brought back to Waset for reburial: but surely in the tomb of her husband in the West Valley. Hence Tomb 55 was never intended for her; and the shrine which was undoubtedly prepared for her was re-used during the burial ceremony of whoever was buried in Tomb 55. It is also easy to imagine that the ephemeral Smenkhkare and his wife, Meretaten, might be buried in the small tomb. If so, then Meretaten's mummy has been removed, although her canopic jars were left behind; whereas Smenkhkare's jars have disappeared, but perhaps his is the body found in the *rishi* coffin. Certainly, Maspero thought so. Perepelkin (*see* above) has argued that the coffin and the canopic jars were prepared for Kiya but remodelled for Akhenaten. However, it is difficult to explain why this should have been necessary. Akhenaten would surely have been buried in his own suite of funerary equipment; and if, several years after his death, his followers had decided to remove his body from the royal tomb at Akhetaten and rebury it in Tomb 55, would they not have left the body of the King in his own coffin for the journey to Waset?

Smenkhkare presumably died in Waset; and it is a reasonable assumption that the coffin prepared for Kiya was in Akhetaten, which begs the question why it was necessary to fetch a coffin to Waset from so far away. In spite of Perepelkin's arguments that Kiya's coffin was altered for Akhenaten, a perhaps more persuasive explanation for the alteration is that given by Fairman,[76] who was convinced that Meretaten was the original owner of the coffin and that it was altered for her husband, Smenkhkare. However, it is a fact that the body in Tomb 55 was found in a coffin that had not been specially made for it; but who was buried in the coffin is the subject of much discussion, and much depends on what age the body had been at death. Elliot Smith estimated the age to be 25 or 26 years, which would rule out Akhenaten, who had fathered at least one child before he came to the throne, and ruled for 17 years. If one assumes that he was about 15 years old when he first became a father, this would make him at least 32 years old when he died. Smenkhkare, on the other hand, could easily have been about 25 years old when he died.

Confirmation of the fact that the skeleton from Tomb 55 was at least that of a male relative of Akhenaten came some 60 years after the tomb was found. In 1969, R.G. Harrison, Professor of Anatomy at the University of Liverpool, and two colleagues, examined the body of Tutankhamun,[77] who had been discovered in 1922 lying undisturbed in his tomb. They found that it was the body of a young male who had been approximately 18 years old when he died. They also found that it showed a remarkable resemblance to the skeleton from Tomb 55, which Harrison had examined in 1963,[78] and that both bodies possessed the identical blood grouping A2MN. In his examination of the skeleton from Tomb 55, Harrison had confirmed that it was that of a male aged 20 to 25 years old at death, thus making it impossible to identify it as that of Akhenaten. The only other candidate who could be linked with the skeleton was Smenkhkare, and it was therefore concluded that the skeleton was his.

Harrison and his colleagues never claimed that the serological data available to them confirmed that Smenkhkare and Tutankhamun were related, let alone brothers. However, it was accepted by many that the fact that they both shared a blood grouping that was apparently relatively rare in ancient Egypt, that they were both members of the royal family of the late Eighteenth Dynasty, that they were both alive at the same time, that they were successive kings and were markedly alike, must surely mean that they were related. To what degree was open to interpretation. The data that 'proved' that they could be brothers could also be used to 'prove' that they were father and son. However, on the basis of the estimated age at death of the body in Tomb 55, it was decided that the most likely relationship was that of siblings. It was thought possible that Amenhotep III could have been the father of both, but very unlikely that Tiye could have been the mother of Tutankhamun since she would have been beyond normal child-bearing age at the time of his birth. Sitamun, the daughter of Amenhotep III and Tiye, was therefore proposed as mother of both Smenkhkare and Tutankhamun. The human remains in Tomb 55 were identified as those of Tutankhamun's brother, Smenkhkare.

In recent years, the wheel has come full circle. Claims[79] have been made that the skeletal remains from Tomb 55 are indeed those of a male, closely related to Tutankhamun: but that the dentition suggests an age in the middle 30s, and anthropological standards and X-rays an age of more than 35 years. Many physical anthropologists dispute these findings, but if they are correct then the remains may be those of Akhenaten after all. The mystery of Tomb 55 has by no means yet been solved.

7. The aftermath of the Amarna Age

Tutankhaten (1336–1327BC) was a child of about eight or nine years old when he became King. Even so, his claim to the throne was consolidated by marriage to Akhenaten's eldest surviving daughter, Ankhesenpaaten, who was a year or two his senior. At the start of the reign, they were living at Akhetaten, probably in the North Palace, but by the second year they had taken up residence at Inebhedj. The palace at Malkata[80] was refurbished for their use during state visits to Upper Egypt, which were largely made so that they could attend religious festivals in Waset. The King and Queen both changed their names, he to Tutankhamun (Living Image of Amun), with the Throne Name Nebkheperure (Master of the Manifestations of Re), and she to Ankhesenamun (May She Live for Amun). These alterations, judging by a number of ring bezels found by archaeologists in the ruins of the workers' village at Akhetaten that bear *cartouches* inscribed with the name Tutankhamun rather than Tutankhaten, must have been made early in the reign whilst the royal couple were still living at Akhetaten. Tutankhamun's highest attested regnal year is 10,[81] which means that he died in his late teens, and might have remained a shadowy and little-known figure in Egyptian history, omitted from the official lists of kings, had it not been for the discovery of his tomb in modern times.

There is a dearth of historical information on the reliefs and statues that survive from Tutankhamun's reign, many of which were usurped by Horemheb, but one important inscription is on the so-called Restoration Stele[82] that was found near the Third Pylon-gateway of the Temple of Amun at Waset. It describes the condition of Egypt when Tutankhamun came to the throne:

> The temples of the gods and goddesses, from Aabu (Aswan) down to the marshes of the Delta, had fallen into decay,
> their shrines had become desolate ruins overgrown with weeds
> and their chapels as though they had never existed. Their halls were used as footpaths. The land was disorderly and the gods turned their backs on it. If agents were despatched to Djahi (Syria) to extend the boundaries of Egypt, they met with no success. If anyone abased himself before a god to petition him, he did not respond; if a prayer was made to a goddess, she did not reply.

The inscription goes on to describe how the King, residing in the palace of Akheperkare (Thutmose I) in Inebhedj, pondered how he might best placate Amun and other deities, and decided that the best way to do it would be to have many statues made for them in gold and precious stones. Thus Tutankhamun became the king who 'spent his life making images of the gods'. He also, according to the Restoration Stele, ordered that the shrines of the gods be repaired, their services re-established, their old priesthoods re-instated and new ones set up. More importantly, the revenues of the temples, which had been sequestered by Akhenaten, were restored to them; and the upkeep for temple musicians and servants became a charge on the royal exchequer.

Since Tutankhamun was a minor when he came to the throne, and, unlike his predecessors, bereft of the advice of influential female members of the royal family such as Tiye, Nefertiti, perhaps even Kiya, who were dead, he must have ruled with the guidance of advisors. The two most important were undoubtedly the Commander-in-Chief of the Army, Horemheb; and Maya, the Treasurer, who should have been under the direction of the Chief Minister of Lower Egypt. During this period, however, little is heard about the holder of this office, or that of Chief Minister of Upper Egypt, normally the most important officials in the kingdom. Although the names of two of Tutankhamun's chief ministers are known — Usermont and Pentu, who may have been the same Pentu who owned a tomb at Akhetaten (*see* p.89) — they do not feature prominently in the records. As Treasurer, Maya was also responsible for the Place of Eternity — the royal necropolis at Waset — and was still active in Horemheb's reign, in the eighth year of which he was in charge of the restoration of the tomb of Thutmose IV, which had been entered illicitly and damaged. An inscription on the south wall of the tomb's antechamber records, in beautiful hieratic (*see* Glossary) handwriting, that 'Maya, son of the noble Iawy, born of the lady of the house, Weret, was charged with the renewal of the burial of King Menkheperure (Thutmose IV)'. Lower down the wall, another inscription mentions 'His assistant, the steward of the southern city, Djehutymose, whose mother is Iniuhe, who belongs to the City (*i.e.* Waset)'.

Maya himself was not buried at Waset but in a splendid tomb at Sakkara, the necropolis of Inebhedj. The Prussian Egyptologist, Karl Richard Lepsius (1810–1884), identified the tomb of Maya in 1843 during his epigraphic mission to record the standing monuments of the Nile Valley; but although several sculptures of various kinds, notably three very fine limestone statues of Maya and his wife, Meryt, had been in the collection of the Rijksmuseum of Leiden in the Netherlands since the 1820s, the site of the tomb was lost until 1975, when it was rediscovered by the British Egyptologist, Geoffrey Martin.[83] As King, Horemheb was eventually buried in the Valley of the Kings, but whilst he was still a general work was begun on a tomb for him at Sakkara, close by Maya's. The decoration of this tomb, which was discovered by Martin in 1975,[84] is largely concerned with Horemheb's military career, notably successful campaigns conducted in Tutankhamun's reign against Syrians and Libyans which resulted in the capture of many prisoners, depicted in fine reliefs on the walls of the tomb. The quality of these and other reliefs leaves no doubt that Horemheb was in a position to employ the finest artists and craftsmen.

Another of Tutankhamun's advisors was Nakhtmin, a military officer who was possibly a son of Ay (*see* below), and therefore the brother or half-brother of Nefertiti, and must himself have been influential at court as an uncle of the Queen; and yet another was Huy, also called Amenhotep, Viceroy of Nubia. In Huy's tomb[85] at Waset finely painted scenes depict representatives of his administrative area, the region from Nekhen (El-Kab) in southern Egypt to Napata, some 500 miles (800km) to the south on the Fourth Cataract of the Nile in the Sudan, presenting Huy with exotic gifts, including a giraffe, and gold. It was the fact that Huy was in charge of an important gold-producing area that made him so powerful, for Egyptian kings used gold to cement alliances with foreign potentates, as a letter from Burraburiash, King of Babylon, to Akhenaten illustrates:

> You have gold in great abundance, so send me as much as your father used to send. If the supply is short, send me half as much as your father used to send ... Three times have your messengers arrived, and you have sent me not a single beautiful present. Therefore, neither have I sent you a beautiful present.[86]

Extensive buiding works were carried out during Tutankhamun's reign, notably at Waset in the Temple of Amun, and in Ipt-rsy (see p.30), where a magnificent set of reliefs depicting the Festival of Opet, the occasion on which Amun paid his annual visit to his southern temple, were carved on the colonnade erected for Amenhotep III. Work was also begun on a tomb (WV23) in the western branch of the Valley of the Kings, near to that of Amenhotep III; and on a memorial temple near Malkata. But before either was completed, Tutankhamun was dead. The cause of his death, at the early age of eighteen or so, is unknown, but modern conspiracy theorists are of the opinion that he was murdered.[87] They base their theory on a small sliver of bone that X-rays have shown lies within Tutankhamun's upper cranial cavity; and on a rounded depression of the left cheek, just in front of the ear lobe: evidence, it is claimed, that he died from a blow to the head. It has been observed that this blow seems to have been aimed from the front, whereas any reasonably competent assassin would surely prefer to strike from behind. X-rays have also revealed that some of Tutankhamun's ribs, and his sternum, are missing, although it is unlikely that these would have been removed during the mummification process. It has been suggested, therefore, that Tutankhamun met with an accident — a fall from his chariot,[88] perhaps into the path of another which staved in his chest.

Howard Carter's discovery on 4th November 1922 of the tomb in the Valley of the Kings in which Tutankhamun's body still lay is one of the most spectacular finds in the history of archaeology and needs no re-telling here. The tomb is small, and resembles that of Yuya and Thuya, and Tomb 55. It was presumably intended originally for a private individual — perhaps Ay (see below) — who was being accorded the honour of burial in the Valley; and Carter identified Maya (see p.123) as its architect. A flight of sixteen steps leads into a descending corridor just over 8 m long, beyond which is the so-called antechamber, a room measuring less than 8m by 3.5, in the far left-hand corner of which is an annexe measuring some 4.5m by 2.5. The ceilings of both rooms are under 3m in height. Beyond the right-hand, or north, wall of the antechamber is the burial chamber, which measures approximately 6.5m by 4 and is less than 4 m high, with another, slightly larger annexe, the so-called Treasury, leading off its north-east corner. The burial chamber is the only part of the tomb that is decorated.

Tutankhamun's tomb was a veritable treasure house, crammed with hundreds of items, many overlaid with gold leaf, thus imprinting on Carter's mind that everywhere he looked 'there was the glint of gold'. Among the treasures were specially-made pieces of funerary equipment, some of which suggest that preparations for Tutankhamun's burial had been underway for some time. The mask (**colour plate 21**) that covered the King's head, made from two separate sheets of gold and inlaid with coloured glass paste and semi-precious stones, is not only of unsurpassed workmanship, the finest mask ever found, it is also a portrait of Tutankhamun. The preparation of the mask, of the magnificent innermost coffin (*see* below) of beaten sheet gold, chased and embellished with inlays, and of the box of the huge sarcophagus (**61**), which measures some 2.75 x 1.45 x 1.47m and was carved from a single block of yellow quartzite, must have been started and completed some years before Tutankhamun's death. The King's unexpected demise, at such an early age, meant that other items of funerary furniture had to be assembled hastily, for the ritual demanded that burial take place seventy days from the time of death.

The lid of the sarcophagus is made of red granite painted yellow in imitation of the box; and Carter suggested that it was perhaps used because it was ready to hand and the quartzite intended for the lid had not yet been obtained. The mismatched lid is cracked. Tutankhamun's body was housed inside three mummy cases, or anthropoid coffins, placed one within the other like a set of Russian dolls. The features of the middle mummy case are different from those of the other two, and this coffin is thought not to have been intended originally for Tutankhamun: it probably belonged to Smenkhkare. The toe of the outer mummy case has been sawn off, suggesting that when the lid of the sarcophagus was first lowered onto the box, the foot of the mummy case protruded above the box, causing the heavy lid to crack. The toe was hastily sheered away, the damage made good with a coating of resin; and the crack in the sarcophagus lid filled in with gypsum, touched up to blend in with the paint.

The four coffinettes in which Tutankhamun's embalmed viscera were placed are miniature copies of the middle mummy case; and it is possible to discern that the inscriptions in the cartouches on the interiors of the coffinette lids originally contained Smenkhkare's Throne Name, Ankhkheperure, which had been excised and Tutankhamun's name written over the top. Carter believed that the lid of one of the coffinettes was ill-fitting and of a poorer standard of workmanship than the rest, which suggests that this coffinette was cobbled together. The coffinettes were placed inside a beautiful calcite shrine with four compartments hollowed out of its interior to accommodate them. Each compartment was topped by four finely-modelled calcite heads, which should have been portraits of Tutankhamun but which do not actually resemble him. The portrait heads may depict Smenkhkare, and the calcite shrine have belonged to him. At least one of the four great nested shrines of gilded wood with which the sarcophagus had been surrounded had certainly been made for him.

Many items of Tutankhamun's funerary equipment seem to have come from a central store of unused royal funerary equipment, or to have been prepared for the reburial at Waset of Akhenaten and Ankhkheperure Neferneferuaten but reinscribed with the name of Tutankhamun. Others were gifts: Maya donated one large *shabti* (*see* Glossary), finely carved in wood, Nakhtmin presented five: all had the donors' names inscribed in

61.   *Tutankhamun: sarcophagus*

hieroglyphs beneath the feet of the *shabties*. Maya also gave a carved effigy of Tutankhamun lying on a lion-headed bier. There were also left-overs from the Atenist period: for example, the figure of the jackel-headed funerary deity, Anubis, which guarded the entrance to the Treasury, was wrapped in a linen shirt that had been marked in ink during Akhenaten's seventh regnal year. What might be termed family mementoes were found in the tomb, notably two ivory scribal palettes that had belonged to Meretaten and Meketaten. Perhaps the most personal memento was found in the Treasury. It had been placed within a tiny mummiform box inside a miniature mummy-case, which was itself housed inside the second of two nested wooden anthropoid coffins. The mummiform box, which is inscribed with the name of Queen Tiye, contained a lock of her hair (**22**), wrapped in linen and anointed with unguents: a precious memento, perhaps, of a beloved grandmother.

It is sometimes speculated that if a minor ruler such as Tutankhamun commanded such a wealth of wonderful funerary objects, how much more splendid must the burials of important kings such as Thutmose III and Ramesses II have been. It is likely, however, that rulers such as these were secure enough in their own greatness not to need a fabulous burial. Indeed, Tutankhamun's tomb seems to be a mixture of objects specially made for him, off-the-peg pieces of equipment, and items obtained by tomb robbery or from the family lumber room, all jumbled up inside his small tomb in an attempt, perhaps, to rid the land of the last vestiges of the reign of Akhenaten. One such vestige is the magnificent chair found in the tomb's antechamber. Called the State Throne (**colour plate 19**), it is made of wood covered with gold leaf; and on its back is an inlaid panel on which the Aten is depicted holding out his rays to the royal couple, who are represented in typical Amarna style. Although certain details on the panel had been altered, the Aten had not been excised from it, evidence, perhaps, that Tutankhamun had not entirely abandoned the god of his childhood, for do not the Jesuits claim that if they are given a child for the first seven years of its life then they will mould the man?

On several items from the tomb, notably a small gold shrine that once housed a statue of Tutankhamun, Queen Ankhesenamun is depicted with her husband. The embossed and chased inner and outer surfaces of the doors and sides of the shrine are decorated in delicate low relief with eighteen small panels depicting, with touching intimacy, episodes from the daily life of the royal couple. In one, for example, Tutankhamun pours perfume into his wife's hand, in another she dabs unguent onto his neck; and in another he is depicted hunting birds, sitting on a stool drawing a bow while she, seated on a cushion at his feet, keeps him supplied with arrows (**colour plate 20**). Carter observed that the dominant note of the scenes was the friendly relationship between husband and wife, 'full of the kindliness which it pleases us to consider modern'.[89]

Mutual support between husband and wife may sometimes have been especially necessary, for two of the most pathetic objects found in the tomb were the mummified remains of two still-born children, assumed to be the offspring of Tutankhamun and Ankhesenamun. They were found in two small anthropoid coffins placed within an undecorated wooden box that lay among several other boxes piled up in the Treasury. One is the foetus of a child, probably a girl, of about fours months development; the other, also probably female, was born prematurely at about seven or eight months.[90] An X-ray of the second child has shown it to have spina bifida, scoliosis (an abnormal curvature of the spine) and an upward displacement of the scapula caused by an inheritable condition known as Sprengel's deformity.[91] Her condition probably means that even if Tutankhamun had lived longer, Ankhesenamun would not have been able to provide him with an heir.

In the event, Tutankhamun died childless; and Ankhesenamun became a widow again, having survived two, perhaps three, husbands. This time, however, she was an adult woman, and as far as the records show, the last of the Thutmoside line: was she tempted to emulate Hatshepsut and declare herself female King of Egypt? That she was prevented from doing so is clear from a scene painted on the wall of Tutankhamun's burial chamber, in which Ay, who was Tutankhamun's relative by marriage but not of the blood royal, is shown conducting the burial rites for the deceased King (**colour plate 22**), thereby claiming his right to the throne. Every reigning King of Egypt was regarded as the living manifestation of Horus, son of Osiris, who had once ruled Egypt but had been murdered by his brother, Seth. Horus legitimated his claim to succeed his father as king by burying him. Thereafter, every dead King of Egypt was regarded as an Osiris; and one of the ways in which a new king legitimized his claim to the throne was by acting as a Horus to his predecessor's Osiris. The new king need not necessarily have been the late king's son, for by the act of burying his predecessor, the new king became in effect his son and heir. Ay could legitimately claim the throne by becoming Horus to Tutankhamun's Osiris.

In what seems like an attempt to prevent Ay becoming king, Ankhesenamun took an unprecedented step. She wrote to Suppiluliuma, King of the Hittites, Egypt's old adversary, telling him of her plight and requesting that he send her one of his sons to be her husband. An account of the correspondence[92] between Ankhesenamun, whom the Hittites refer to as Dakhamun, and Suppiluliuma was given by his son, Mursilis II, and stored on a clay tablet in the archives of the Hittite capital city, Hattusas. Mursilis describes how his father attacked Amka (the region of Antioch in Syria), terrifying the Egyptians; and goes on:

> Then their ruler, Bibkhururiyas (Nebkheperure *i.e.* Tutankhamun), just at that moment died. Now the Queen of Egypt was Dakhamun ... she sent an emissary to my father, and said to him: 'My husband is dead. I have no children. Your sons are said to be grown up. If you will give me one of your sons, he will be my husband, he will be of help to me. Send him forthwith and thereafter I will make him my husband and send bridal gifts.'

Suppiluliuma distrusted the Queen's intent and sent a secretary to Egypt with instructions to bring back a report on why she had written the letter and on what had become of 'the son of their (the Egyptians') ruler'.
Mursilis goes on:

> When the secretary had returned from Egypt — it was after this that my father captured the city of Carchemish, which he had besieged for seven days, and on the eighth day battled all day and on the eight and ninth days

he stormed the city ... and captured the city thereafter ... my father sent a secretary to the land of Egypt (to ask): 'Where is the son of their lord? Is she deceiving me? Surely the general of the army is not promoting my son to the kingship!'

Ankhesenamun, who had only seventy days between Tutankhamun's death and the day of his burial, when whoever buried him would claim the throne of Egypt, must have become somewhat fraught by now at the wily old king's procrastination. She sent another letter:

What is this you say: 'She is deceiving me.' If I had a son ... would I have written. But I have no son. And now you say to me: 'Where is your husband?' He is dead and I have no son. Should I take a servant? I have not written to any other country on this matter, I have only written to you. Your sons are said to be grown up. Send me one of your sons, and he shall be my husband and King of Egypt.

At last, according to Mursilis, 'the lady's request was fulfilled'; and one of his brothers, Zennanza, was selected to be her husband.

The reason for Ankhesenamun's desperate action may have been that she preferred to become the consort of a foreign prince rather demean herself by marrying one of her Egyptian subjects, especially if that subject were Ay, her own grandfather (*see* below). On the other hand, she may have been attempting to ally herself with Suppiluliuma, at that time the most powerful foreign ruler, in order to save Egypt from him. After all, if Mursilis is to be believed, the Egyptians were 'terrified' when his father attacked Amka. Whatever the reason for Ankhesenamun's action, it was to no avail. Suppiluliuma sent Zennanza to Egypt but without troops in sufficient numbers to protect him. The unfortunate Zennanza was met on the borders of Egypt by a contingent of the Egyptian army and killed — presumably on the orders of General Horemheb. Thus Suppiluliuma missed his great opportunity to ally himself with Egypt; and the course of history was changed. If Zennanza had become King of Egypt, both Egypt and Hatti would have been spared years of warfare.

Zennanza may have been replaced as Ankhesenamun's bridegroom by Ay. In 1931, Percy Newberry (1869–1949), who had been Professor of Egyptology at the University of Liverpool between 1906 and 1919, examined a blue glass ring then in the possession of a dealer in antiquities in Cairo. He claimed that engraved on its bezel were the *cartouches* of Ay and Ankhesenamun, side by side, the usual way of indicating a marriage, suggesting that Ay had married his grand-daughter. Whether or not such a marriage took place, Ay (1327–1323BC) became King of Egypt, with the Throne Name Kheperkheperure (Everlasting are the Manifestations of Re); and Ankhesenamun disappeared from history. There are few surviving monuments from his short reign, most having been usurped by Horemheb, including the memorial temple near Malkata that had been erected over an earlier structure built for Tutankhamun. Two quartzite colossi of Tutankhamun that had stood in his memorial temple were usurped by Ay; but even these were later usurped by Horemheb. The large tomb (WV23) that Ay had prepared for himself had originally

62.   *Horemheb: relief from his Sakkara tomb*

belonged to Tutankhamun. Its walls were extensively painted; and in the burial chamber one painting in particular is noteworthy, for it shows Ay, accompanied by his first wife, Tey, fowling in the marshes and spearing a hippopotamus, scenes that are unique in a royal tomb. When the tomb was opened in AD1816, Ay's red granite sarcophagus had been smashed into pieces, although its domed lid was discovered intact amid the debris on the burial chamber floor in 1972. Of Ay, however, there was no sign.

Ay was succeeded by the Commander-in-Chief of the Army, Horemheb (**62**), undoubtedly with the full support of an army that had decided it was time to intervene before the political situation in Egypt became irretrievable and the whole Asiatic empire was lost. Thus, not for the last time in the ancient or modern world, did the army take control when it deemed that civilian governance had been a failure. Nevertheless, Horemheb (1323–1295BC), who took the Throne Name Djeserkheperure-Setepenre (Holy are the Manifestations of Re-Chosen of Re), took the precaution of marrying Mutnodjmet, Nefertiti's sister and as such the last link with the old royal family.

Little is known about Horemheb's antecedents. His family came from Henen-nesut (modern Ihnasya el-Medina, known to the Greeks as Herakleopolis), a town on the edge of the Faiyum in which the chief deity was the ram-headed god, Herishef. He may have had quite lowly origins for there is no suggestion that his family were of sufficient importance to have played any part in the local cult. Nevertheless, Horemheb must have been a talented and forceful man who, like other Egyptians of his era who were not from influential families, rose to prominence through the ranks of the army. He first served during the reign of Amenhotep III, became Commander-in-Chief under Akhenaten, and was appointed King's Deputy by Tutankhamun. Thus he must have been well into his fifties when he came to the throne.

Although Horemheb had been instrumental in endeavours to safeguard the empire long before he became king, his reign was one of consolidation and the restoration of the *status quo ante* the reign of Akhenaten. It was also a time of rebuilding and of expunging from Egyptian annals all memory of 'that criminal of Akhetaten' and his successors, whom he considered tainted with the Atenist heresy. He held no truck with any of the four previous kings and dated his reign from the death of Amenhotep III. Horemheb was an efficient and successful king: he was wise enough not to let the priesthood of Amun regain the power they had had up to the reign of Amenhotep III, and appointed 'the pick of the army' as priests. He also determined that no army commander should challenge him and therefore weakened their positions by dividing the army under two commanders, one for Upper, the other for Lower, Egypt. In place of palace favourites such as stewards and fan bearers, to whom his predecessors had delegated much of their royal authority, he restored full judicial power to the Chief Ministers of Upper and Lower Egypt.

A magnificent tomb (KV57) was cut for Horemheb, one of the largest in the Valley of the Kings, chiefly decorated with sculpted reliefs rather than scenes painted on plaster in the manner of earlier tombs. The great red granite sarcophagus was empty when the tomb was discovered by Theodore Davis in AD1908, and Horemheb's mummy has not yet been found. Although Horemheb was never to use the tomb he had prepared for himself at Sakkara, at a time when he could have had no thought of becoming king, in many of the reliefs he wears the uraeus (*see* Glossary), proving that he must have sent his workmen to add this symbol of royalty after his elevation to the throne. His Queen, Mutnodjmet, was not granted the privilege of burial with her husband: she was buried in the tomb at Sakkara, alongside Horemheb's first wife, whose name seems to have been Amenia.

Horemheb appears to have had no living son by either wife. The broken remains of the body of a woman were found at the edge of a burial shaft in Horemheb's tomb at Sakkara.[93] The skull and the pelvis have been analysed and prove to be those of a woman who had given birth several times; and who had lost all her teeth early in life, necessitating that her diet consisted mainly of soft foods. The bones of a newborn child, or possibly a foetus, were buried with her, suggesting that she had died in childbirth. If, as seems likely, the adult bones belong to Mutnodjmet, then she may have died in yet another futile attempt to give her husband an heir. Horemheb was thus forced to appoint as his successor an elderly fellow-general, Pramessu, who became king as Ramesses I (1295–1294 BC). With him a new line of kings began, although the rulers of this, the Nineteenth Dynasty, looked upon Horemheb as its true founder. Many of their officials honoured him likewise and chose to be buried around his tomb at Sakkara: even Princess Tia, the sister of Ramesses the Great, elected to have her tomb built there. As for their opinion of Akhenaten and all his works, it might best be summed up in the following brief extract from Agatha Christie's *Akhnaten* (*see* p.45):

TYE: Besides, you are the only man near my son with the least ability. He surrounds himself with painters and dancers and sculptors — and not a scrap of brains between them!

HOREMHEB (*speaking with immense contempt*): Soft. A soft lot!

Or were they?

8. The uncovering of Amarna

A Brief History of its Archaeological Excavations

The first European known to have visited Amarna in modern times was Sir John Gardner Wilkinson (1797–1875), the English Egyptologist, who was also the first to use the title Tell el-Amarna. He made two visits to the site, the first in 1824, the second two years later, accompanied by another Egyptologist, James Burton (1788–1862), a gifted draughtsman. At the time of Wilkinson's visits, the tombs cut into the northern cliffs were readily accessible, and copies were made of the sculptured scenes which decorated the walls of one of them, that belonging to Meryre (*see* p.88). The tombs cut into the southern cliffs were choked with sand, but in 1833, Robert Hay (1799–1863), the great Scottish draughtsman and copyist, had several cleared so that copies of their reliefs could be made. In the tombs, reliefs depicting the activities of two figures with swelling breasts, narrow waists, rounded hips and thighs and delicate calves, features considered to be pronouncedly female, intrigued the investigators. They raised questions — if the figures represented a king accompanied by his wife, as might be expected, why were both so effeminate? Or were the figures those of two queens?

The copies made by Hay are stored in the British Library, and most of them, sadly, are unpublished. A similar fate has befallen the work of the French draughtsman, Nestor L'Hôte (1804–1842), who was invited to accompany Jean-François Champollion as his draughtsman when the great philologist made his first visit to Egypt in 1828, six years after he had published his decipherment of hieroglyphs. The notes, water colours, drawings and papier mâché squeezes made by L'Hôte not only at El-Amarna but at many other sites are housed, largely unpublished, either in the Louvre or in the Bibliothèque Nationale in Paris. And so, although reports of what could be seen at El-Amarna intrigued those who were unable to visit the site, it was not until 1859 that comprehensive drawings and plans became available to them.

Between 1842 and 1845, Richard Lepsius (*see* p.123) led the Prussian Expedition to Egypt and Nubia. He paid two visits to El-Amarna, in 1843 and 1845, and over a period of twelve days produced an enormous amount of very fine drawings and squeezes. These, together with material collected during the Expedition from sites all over Egypt and Nubia, were published in 1859 in the twelve huge volumes of the *Denkmäler*, perhaps the largest work on Egyptology ever produced. The drawings in the *Denkmäler* are extremely accurate compared with those in earlier works; and for the rest of the century scholars studying El-Amarna depended upon them for information on scenes and inscriptions not only in the tombs but also on some of the great stelae that delineated the boundaries of the city and its outlying district (*see* p.79).

Meantime, it had become clear that in the years following Napoleon's 1798 Expedition to Egypt, which brought ancient Egypt to the attention of Europe and America, Egyptian antiquities had been torn up wholesale and shipped to museums and private collections all over the world. Finally, however, Said Pasha, Viceroy of Egypt, became persuaded of the advantages of preserving Egypt's heritage and, in 1858, appointed the French scholar, Auguste Mariette (1821–1881), first director of the newly-created Office of Antiquities and chief supervisor of excavations. In that same year Mariette set up a museum at Boulaq, near Cairo, to house Egyptian antiquities; and stipulated that not only did anyone wishing to work on archaeological sites have to have a permit to do so but everything they discovered had to be offered to the Egyptian Museum. Thus Mariette went a long way towards halting the plunder and unrestrained sale of Egyptian antiquities. Scientific archaeologists welcomed the restrictions, but even they had to hope that the Museum would allow them a reasonable proportion of the objects they discovered so that they would have something with which to reward their backers or to sell in order to finance further excavations.

In the forty years following Lepsius's work not much scholarly attention was paid to Tell el-Amarna: but in 1885, a peasant woman digging at the site for *sebakh*, the organic debris, rich in nitrogen, into which ancient mud-brick decomposes and which is used as fertilizer, unearthed a pile of nearly 400 small slabs (tablets) made of baked clay and inscribed with wedge-shaped symbols. She is said to have sold them to a local man for 10 piastres (about two pence today), who then sold them on to a dealer who, uncertain what to make of them, consulted experts in Cairo and Paris, notably the French Assyriologist, Jules Oppert (1825–1905). They were pronounced fakes; and for several months were hawked up and down Egypt grinding against each other in a sack.

In 1887, E.A. Wallis Budge (1857–1934) visited Egypt as a representative of the British Museum. The new Director of the Egyptian Antiquities Service, Eugène Grébaut (1846–1915), warned him on pain of arrest against buying antiquities, but in spite of Grébaut's threat, Budge bought the magnificent Papyrus of Ani from the antique dealer, Muhammad Mohassib Bey (1843–1928). There is a story,[94] which may be apocryphal, that while Budge was in Mohassib Bey's house in Luxor, the police surrounded it and waited for Grébaut to arrive from Cairo to arrest him. Fortunately for Budge, the boat on which Grébaut was travelling grounded — amazingly, near the place where the pilot's daughter was due to be married next day — thus delaying Grébaut's arrival. Budge was allowed to return to his hotel, and it too was surrounded by police, although a man managed to get through the police cordon to offer Budge six of the clay tablets that had been found at El-Amarna. Luckily, Budge recognized that the inscriptions on the tablets were in cuneiform, the script used in ancient Mesopotamia and Assyria; and were written in Akkadian, the international diplomatic language of the second millennium BC. 'I felt certain,' he said later, 'that the tablets were both genuine and of very great historical importance.' He bought them; and before long, a second man had slipped through the police cordon with 76 more tablets.

Budge was faced with the problem of getting the tablets from El-Amarna and his other purchases back to England. They were stored in a small house built against the garden wall of his hotel; and the hotel gardeners agreed to tunnel through to the house and smuggle them out whilst the hotel manager distracted the police guard with a free meal. When Budge finally arrived in Cairo, it was late at night and he could not find transport for his luggage, which, of course, contained the forbidden antiquities. He managed to persuade Grébaut's police to transport it to the British Army barracks; and eventually, the army shipped home Budge's collection, not least the eighty-two tablets from El-Amarna that are now in the British Museum. The Germans had been even more successful than Budge in obtaining what remained of the tablets, and managed to smuggle 160 to Berlin. Over the next few years, more tablets were found; and today there are 382 surviving tablets in London, Berlin, Paris and St Petersburg, and in several private collections. Sadly, thanks to the cavalier way in which the majority of these dull-looking objects had first been handled, 'What has been preserved is but a wreck of what might have been.'[95]

Nevertheless, scholars studying the tablets from El-Amarna soon realized that they were a sensational find. They proved to be the diplomatic correspondence between the rulers of Palestine and Syria and the Kings of Egypt dating from the period around 1355 to 1335BC, and include letters from rulers and copies of the replies sent in return; and dispatches sent back to Egypt by Egyptian emissaries. Although largely written in Akkadian, the language of central Mesopotamia in the second millennium BC, with one or two letters in Assyrian, Hurrian or Hittite, they contain a number of Egyptian words relating to administrative or military matters and names of objects requested from Egypt.

After the value of the Amarna Letters (**63**) had been recognized, excavations were undertaken at the site in which they had been found by, amongst others, Grébaut. At the end of October 1891, W.M. Flinders Petrie arrived in Cairo, excited by the thought of finding more cuneiform tablets, and in the hope of eliciting information about the king whose name, deciphered by Egyptologists as 'Khuenaten' rather than Akhenaten, appeared in inscriptions in the tombs at El-Amarna. He applied to Grébaut, in his capacity of Director of the Antiquities Service, for a permit to excavate. Considering that to ask outright for Tell el-Amarna would only lead the awkward Director to refuse, Petrie first asked for Sakkara or Abydos, confident that they would be denied him. Grébaut graciously offered him what he supposed was Petrie's third choice, El-Amarna — not the tombs which, he said, were already being worked on, but the city area.

Petrie set off for El-Amarna, stopping on the way at Illahun in the Faiyum to persuade five of his best workmen from his previous season's dig at Meidum to come with him. On arrival at the site, which he called 'The City of Khuenaten', priority was given to the construction of a shelter for themselves. The Egyptians made the 3000 mud-bricks it took to build a three-room house; and Petrie himself was the bricklayer. Once the house was built, he inspected what he called his 'heritage': a city site, as Petrie said, that was about the size of Brighton, and would take a lifetime to excavate; even to plan the whole area was a daunting task. Armed with the plan that Lepsius had drawn in the 1840s, Petrie walked over the area trying to identify the mounds but looking in particular for temples and the royal palace; and for houses so that he might reconstruct a typical house plan.

Petrie took on forty more workmen and began to excavate and plan many of the official buildings in the central area of the city. He identified the remains of one building as the palace because of its size and the fact that it had a large hall with emplacements for over 500 columns. In another hall he uncovered what he pronounced to be the most important

63   *Amarna Letter: from Tushratta of Mitanni to Amenhotep III [from J. Baikie, The Amarna
Age, London, 1926, Pl.VI]*

discovery artistically since the Old Kingdom statues discovered by Mariette: a floor, measuring about 250 square feet, made of brightly painted plaster on which was depicted a lake surrounded with reeds through which pintail ducks flew up into the air and calves kicked up their heels. Petrie sent immediately to the Office of Works requesting funding for building a roof over the floor. The letter was passed to Grébaut who ignored it. Meanwhile, Petrie constructed a walkway around the floor so that visitors, whom he correctly supposed would come rushing to see it once the news of its discovery got out, could view it without inflicting damage. He also took steps to preserve it by very gently applying, with his forefinger, a thin coating of tapioca mixed with water. A shed was eventually erected over the floor to protect it, but some twenty years after its discovery it was destroyed in an act of wanton vandalism. A local farmer, sick of the hordes of tourists who trampled through his fields to reach it, hacked the plaster to pieces.[96]

In his six months at El-Amarna, Petrie was to discover another artistic masterpiece in the king's private residence — a fragment of an exquisite wall-painting showing two little princesses playing at the feet of their mother.[97] His most valuable discoveries, however, came from the ancient city's refuse dumps which, in true Petrie fashion, he sifted through with great care. His study of inscriptions on broken jars that had once held wine or oil enabled him to build up a picture of places of origin and dates of shipments. More importantly, dockets on wine jars giving the date of the vintage enabled him to work out the length of the reign of 'Khuenaten': the current view was that the king had reigned for twelve years: Petrie proved that he had died in, or just after, the seventeenth year of his reign. Less than two years after his season at El-Amarna, Petrie was to publish what was, in the opinion of John Pendlebury (*see* p.140), 'one of the most useful books on the site ever written.'[98]

In 1901, the Egypt Exploration Fund of London applied to Gaston Maspero (1846–1916), who had been appointed Director-General of the Antiquities Service for a second time two years previously, for permission to copy the reliefs in the private tombs at El-Amarna. Maspero readily agreed; and Norman de Garis Davies (1865–1941), the Fund's Surveyor, spent six to eight weeks in each of the next six years copying all the decorated and inscribed private tombs as well as the Boundary Stelae. The results of his work — and it was largely Davies's work — were published in the six volumes of *The Rock Tombs of El-Amarna*, which contain a wealth of detail of life in Akhetaten retrieved from tomb walls that were 'unfinished, decaying, damaged and often filthy from infestation by generations of bats and human squatters'.[99]

Petrie's discoveries at El-Amarna were overshadowed by those of the German Expedition which excavated there largely under the direction of Ludwig Borchardt (1863–1938) from 1907 until the outbreak of the First World War. During the 1911 season, the Germans had begun to excavate an area of the Main City around the easternmost of its three great streets, which they named the Street of the High Priests. Judging from what had been found on the south western side of the street the area had been one in which builders, artisans and artists had their houses and workshops. On the first day of the 1912 season, 25th November, an unfinished statue was found: made of limestone, it represents a king in the act of kissing a child whom he holds on his knee. The same house yielded several more heads and busts; and an ivory horse blinker was unearthed from a pit in the courtyard. An inscription on the blinker referred to 'the Chief of Works, the Sculptor, Thutmose';[100] and it was assumed that Thutmose was not only the owner of the house but was also the sculptor responsible for producing these fine works of art.[101] The identification also made him one of the very few ancient Egyptian artists whose name is known.

On December 6, Borchardt's foreman, Mohammed, removed the debris covering a life-sized bust lying head down in the sand in the far left-hand corner of the room he was clearing. Hermann Ranke (1878–1953), the Egyptologist in charge, sent for Borchardt, who used his hands to sweep the debris away from the head, which was lying with its face turned towards the wall. Gradually, the chin, the nose and the face emerged, then the large, distinctive headdress. Once the 48 cm high bust was free of the debris which had covered it, the three men beheld a richly painted, almost perfectly intact, limestone bust of the queen whose timeless beauty has transcended the ages — Nefertiti (**64 and colour plate 9**). The bust, Thutmose's masterpiece, has become the best-known work of art from ancient Egypt.

Contrary to his usual practice, Borchardt stayed up until after midnight writing up the day's events. He gave up trying to describe the bust with the words: 'Description is no use; observation!' — a statement that is equally valid today. Borchardt puzzled over why the bust was so well preserved. The explanation seems to be that it had been placed on a wooden shelf in a small chamber adjoining Thutmose's living room, and when Akhetaten was abandoned the bust was left behind. The years passed, the room filled with blown sand and the wood either rotted or was eaten by termites until finally the shelf tipped over, and the bust, top heavy because of the weight of the headdress, fell into the sand head down, face turned towards the wall. There it lay, as more and more debris covered it, until it was discovered by the foreman, Mohammed.

Borchardt did not rush to tell the world, much less the Egyptian Antiquities Service, of the wonderful find. Instead, he wrote to Maspero asking him to come to El-Amarna to examine the season's finds, none of which, he assured him, was remarkable. There were a few that he would like to send to Berlin for study purposes, but of course would need Maspero's permission to do so. Maspero decided that he need not visit the site himself and despatched a young assistant. He could find no objects that were suitable for display in Cairo Museum; and signed papers for five crates containing 'a few baskets of clay shards and many limestone fragments.' One of the crates may have contained a spectacular 'limestone fragment' — the bust of Nefertiti — but its presence in Germany was not acknowledged until 1920 when it resurfaced in the Berlin Museum.

Naturally, the Egyptian authorities were curious as to how the bust had made its way to Berlin. Borchardt claimed that on January 20, 1913, he had made an agreement with Maspero that the bust of Nefertiti should be allotted to Berlin. Maspero could not confirm the unlikely story, since he had died in 1916; but the Antiquities Service did not believe a word of it and issued an ultimatum — return the bust or German archaeologists will be denied any further access to Egyptian sites. After many years, German Egyptologists were allowed back into Egypt; but the bust of Nefertiti remains in Berlin Museum.

In 1920, the Egypt Exploration Society of London renewed its concession to excavate at El-Amarna. Although funds were curtailed by the Great Depression in the 1930s, the Society managed to finance fifteen seasons, the results of which were published each year in the *Journal of Egyptian Archaeology*, and in the three volumes of the excavation memoirs, *The City of Akhenaten*. T. E. Peet (1882–1934), Brunner Professor of Egyptology in Liverpool University, was appointed Director of the initial season of excavations, in spite of the fact that he was a philologist rather than an archaeologist. He was succeeded the following year by Leonard Woolley (1880–1960), who after a fruitful season's work departed for Mesopotamia, to become famous for his excavations at Ur, undertaken between 1922–1934. An architect, Francis Newton (1878–1924), who had been working at El-Amarna since 1920, making the plans and drawings of vast areas of the city that are the glory of the first volume of *The City of Akhenaten*, took over from Woolley as Director. Sadly, the 1924 season was to be Newton's last: he was taken ill on site and died in Assiut on Christmas Day.

During the first half of the 1920s, great attention was paid to the uncovering of the large private houses in the Main City that had been begun by the Germans. The most important of the mansions excavated was that belonging to the Chief Minister, Nakht, with its reception halls, bedrooms and bathrooms (*see* p.82). In addition, the village that had housed the men employed to construct the tombs was identified and partially excavated. Woolley took a special interest in an area to the south of the city where Alexandre Barsanti (1858–1917), an Alexandrian of Italian origin employed by the Cairo Museum as a restorer, had found fragments of a fine painted pavement which he removed to Cairo. Woolley was able to demonstrate that the pavement had belonged to the Maru-Aten.

In the area north of the modern village of Et-Til, the Egypt Exploration Society excavators discovered the mud-brick walls, surviving in places up to a height of 2m, of a great palace. The walls of one of the rooms in this, the Northern Palace, were plastered and painted with scenes of bird-life in the marshes; but the plaster was in such a fragile state that it was in danger of collapse. Newton (*see* above) set about recording the scenes; and two years after his death, Norman de Garis Davies, returning to El-Amarna accompanied by his equally talented wife, Nina (1881–1965), completed the task. Their facsimiles, and some of the late Director's own beautiful coloured drawings, were published in 1929 as a memorial volume to Newton.[102]

In 1926, with the Dutch Egyptologist, Henri Frankfort (1897–1954), as Director, work began on excavating the huge, much-ruined, Great Temple of the Aten — but the excavation of private houses was not neglected. The house belonging to the Chief Servitor of the Aten, Panehsy (*see* p.90), whose tomb in the northern group was already known, was identified. Like several of the other houses, Panehsy's had a small chapel attached to it. Normally these chapels were dedicated to the worship of the royal family: but a limestone stele[103] found in Panehsy's house depicted Akhenaten's father and mother rather than Akhenaten himself (*see* p.53).

For six fruitful seasons, from 1931 to 1936, when the concession was relinquished, the post of Field Director at El-Amarna was held by John Pendlebury (1904–1941), a specialist in Cretan archaeology who had already been appointed Curator of Knossos in succession to Sir Arthur Evans (1851–1941), the discoverer of the Minoan civilization. Pendlebury was to spend the next few years excavating in Crete during the summer months and at El-Amarna in the winter. During that time the central city was cleared and re-examined, and important official buildings as well as many houses excavated. With the help of Ralph Lavers, Pendlebury was able to reconstruct the layout and a large part of the groundplan of the great Aten temple and the main palace. In addition, he located the records office and other administrative buildings. One of his most important archaeological contributions was his study and classification of objects showing contacts between the Aegean and Egypt. Pendlebury contributed to the second volume of *The City of Akhenaten*; but the two parts of the third volume, containing the reports of his work on the central city and the official buildings, were published posthumously, edited by H.W. Fairman and others, in 1951.

The six years that Pendlebury spent at El-Amarna today seem like the golden age of excavations at the site. This was due in part to his own personality, which is fondly remembered and brought to life by his friends: Mary Chubb, in *Nefertiti Lived Here*, first published in 1954 and republished in 1999; and the film critic, Dilys Powell, in *The Villa Ariadne* (1973). In 1939, Pendlebury joined the 18th Infantry Brigade in Crete as Captain; and in May 1941, he was severely wounded in action. Gravely ill, he was taken from his sickbed and interrogated by the Germans on the position of the British forces. He refused to answer their questions and was shot, possibly on 24th May, 1941. His death was a loss to Egyptology, not least because it prevented the detailed report on his work at El-Amarna which only his first-hand experience could have produced.

A team of young, enthusiastic, Egyptologists, all still in their twenties, had been assembled under Pendlebury. One of them, who appears in *Nefertiti Lived Here* under the sobriquet of Tommy, was Herbert Fairman, who, according to Mary Chubb, was at his happiest when 'funny little bits of baked clay and shards' were brought to him, 'so long as they had inscriptions or fragments of inscriptions on them.' It is ironic that Fairman, a noted philologist, should have been the one to make the great artistic discovery of the Pendlebury years. He used to tell the tale of how he was sent to El-Amarna to start off the season's excavations in the private houses in an area of the southern city; and had the great good fortune to uncover the unfinished, life-sized, quartzite bust of Nefertiti, still with the sculptor's guidelines painted on it, that is now one of the treasures of the Cairo Museum (**65**). He also confessed that his euphoria at the discovery was so great that he could not resist seeing how Nefertiti looked wearing his beret.

In 1931, the Egyptian Antiquities Service had asked the Egypt Exploration Society to re-examine the area around the Royal Tomb, which was situated in the *Wadi* Abu Hasah. The tomb had first been cleared and examined by Barsanti in 1891; and some of its much-damaged reliefs and inscriptions recorded two years later by the Mission archéologique française. In 1935, the Egypt Exploration Society was given permission to record and publish all of the reliefs and inscriptions in the tomb. Fairman and Lavers were principally concerned with the task of making tracings of and photographing the walls; and Pendlebury was able to publish a brief report of their work.[104] It was to be 54 years, however, before the Royal Tomb was published in full as volume seven of *The Rock Tombs of El-Amarna*.[105]

64.   *Nefertiti: bust, painted limestone (Ägyptisches Museum, Berlin)*

65)   Nefertiti: head, red quartzite (Egyptian Museum, Cairo)

In 1977, when the Egypt Exploration Society resumed excavating at Tell el-Amarna, it was decided that priority should be given to the making of a map showing in detail the sites that had been uncovered over the years, something which at that time was sadly lacking. In only two seasons, Barry Kemp produced a 1:2,500 scale map of the main city site; and a 1:5,000 map of the entire area. At the same time, a small stone village was brought to light 2km to the south-west of the opening of the Royal *Wadi*; and investigations were undertaken at a place to the south of the main city, known as *Kom el-Nana* (the Mound of Mint) and designated by Petrie as a 'Roman Camp'. Kemp came to the conclusion that the stone village had probably been made for the overnight accommodation of workmen engaged on the preparation of the private tombs; and that the so-called Roman Camp in fact dates to Akhenaten's reign and was at least in part a bakery and brewery for the preparation of special festival foods.

Work goes on at Tell el-Amarna, a site that has not yet given up all of its secrets. It continues to excite the imagination, for Amarna has become the byword for the age of political turmoil and religious and artistic revolution that shook Egypt in the mid-fourteenth century BC.

Bibliography and further reading

There are a great many books and scholarly papers written about the Amarna Age: they are conveniently indexed in G.T. Martin, *A Bibliography of the Amarna Period and its Aftermath: The Reigns of Akhenaten, Smenkhkare, Tutankhamun and Ay*, London, 1991

Abbreviations

AL   *Amarna Letters: Essays on Ancient Egypt c.1390–1310 BC* (San Francisco)
ANET   J.B. Pritchard (ed.), *Ancient Near Eastern Texts relating to the Old Testament*, 3rd ed., Princeton, 1969
ARE   J.H. Breasted, *Ancient Records of Egypt*, Chicago, 1906
CAH   Cambridge Ancient History
JEA   *Journal of Egyptian Archaeology*
JNES   *Journal of Near Eastern Studies*
KMT   [A Modern Journal of Ancient Egypt], (Sebastopol, California)

Introduction

Clayton, P.A. *Chronicle of the Pharaohs*, London, 1994.
Gardiner, A.H. *Egypt of the Pharaohs*, Oxford, 1961
Grimal, N. *A History of Ancient Egypt*, Oxford, 1992
Hayes, W.C. *Egypt: Internal affairs from Tuthmosis I to the death of Amenophis III*, CAH, Vol.II, Chapter IX: 1 & 2, 1962

1 The rise of Amen-Re, King of the Gods

Breasted, J.H. *Ancient Records of Egypt,* Chicago, 1906.
Hayes, W.C. 'The power of Amun', in *Egypt: Internal affairs from Tuthmosis I to the death of Amenophis III*, CAH, Vol.II, Chapter IX: 1, 1962, pp.13-19.

2 Amenhotep III, Egypt's Sun King

Blankenburg-van Delden, C. *The Large Commemorative Scarabs of Amenhotep III, Leiden,* 1969
Bryan, B.M. *The Reign of Thutmose IV*, Baltimore, 1991

Davis, T.D., et al. *The Tomb of Iouiya and Touiyou*, London, 1907. See also AL, Volume One, 1991, pp.4-25

Forbes, D.C. *Royal Mummies Musical Chairs: Cases of Mistaken Identities?* in KMT, 10 (1), 1999, pp.77-83

Gohary, J. *Guide to the Nubian Monuments on Lake Nasser*, Cairo, 1998

Harris, J.E. *Who's Who in Room 52?* in KMT, 1 (2), 1990, pp.38-42

Johnson, G.B. *Yuya's Mummy Mask*, in KMT, 7 (2), 1996, pp.40-45

Johnson, W.R. *Images of Amenhotep III in Thebes: Styles and Intentions,* in *The Art of Amenhotep III: Art Historical Analysis*, Indiana University Press, 1990

Kitchen, K.A. *Suppiluliuma and the Amarna Pharaohs: A Study in Relative Chronology*, Liverpool, 1962

Knudtzon, J.A. *Die El-Amarna-Tafeln*, Anmerkingen und Register bearbeitet von O. Weber und E. Ebeling, 2 vols, Leipzig, 1907–1915

Kozloff, A.P. and Bryan, B.M. *Egypt's Dazzling Sun: Amenhotep III and His World*, Indiana University Press, 1992

Murnane, W.J. *Amenhotep, Son of Hapu*, in KMT, 2 (2), 1991, p.8 foll.

Partridge, R.B. *Faces of Pharaohs: Royal Mummies and Coffins from Ancient Thebes*, London, 1994

Quibell, J. *Tomb of Yuaa and Thuiu*, Cairo, 1908

Reeves, N. & Wilkinson, R.H. *The Complete Valley of the Kings: Tombs and Treasures of Egypt's Greatest Pharaohs*, London, 1996

Sethe, K. & Helck, W. *Urkunden der 18. Dynastie (Urk. IV)*. 22 vols, Leipzig and Berlin, 1906–58

3 Akhenaten and Nefertiti

Aldred, C. *Akhenaten and Nefertiti*, New York, 1973

Aldred, C. *Akhenaten, King of Egypt*, London, 1988

Aldred, C. *Akhenaten, Pharaoh of Egypt — A New Study*, London, 1968

Aldred, C. *Egypt: The Amarna Period and the end of the Eighteenth Dynasty*, in CAH, Vol. II, Chapter XIX, 1971

Allen, J.P. *Akhenaten's 'Mystery' Coregent and Successor*, in AL, Volume One, 1991, pp.74-85

Breasted, J.H. *Ikhnaton, the Religious Revolutionary*. Chapter 6 of J.B. Bury et al., eds, CAH, 1st ed., Vol.2, 1924, pp.109-30

Dodson, A. *Crown Prince Djhutmose and the Royal Sons of the Eighteenth Dynasty*, in JEA, 76, 1990, pp.87-96

Fairman, H.W. *Once Again the So-called Coffin of Akhenaten*, in JEA, 47, 1961, pp.25-40

Gardiner, A.H. *The Graffito from the Tomb of Pere*, in JEA, 14, 1928, pp.10-11, pls 5,6

Harris, J.E. et al. *Mummy of the 'Elder Lady' in the Tomb of Amenhotep II: Egyptian Museum Catalog Number 61070*, in *Science*, 200, 9 June 1978, pp.1149-51

Harris, J.R. *Neferneferuaten Regnans*, in *Acta Orientalia*, 36, 1974, pp.11-21

Hayes, W.C. *The Scepter of Egypt: A Background for the Study of the Egyptian Antiquities in the Metropolitan Museum of Art*, Part 2, New York, 1959

Johnson, G.B. *Seeking Queen Nefertiti's Tall Blue Crown*, in AL, Volume One, 1991, pp.50-61

Knudtzon, J.A., et al. *Die El-Amarna-Tafeln*, 2 vols, Leipzig, 1908–15

Martin, G.T. *The Royal Tomb at el-'Amarna*. 2 vols. Pt 7 of The Rock Tombs of el-'Amarna, London, 1974, 1989

Moran, W.L. *The Amarna Letters*, Baltimore, 1992

Murnane, W.J. *Texts from the Amarna Period in Egypt*, Atlanta,1995

Reeves, C.N. *New Light on Kiya from Texts in the British Museum*, in JEA, 74, 1988, pp.91-101

Roeder, G. *Amarna-Blocke aus Hermopolis*, Hildesheim, 1969

Smith, R.W. & Redford, D.B. *Initial Discoveries:The Akhenaten Temple Project*, Vol.1. Warminster, 1976

Thomas, A.P. *The Other Woman at Akhetaten: Royal Wife Kiya*, in AL, Volume Three, 1994, pp.72-81

Tyldesley, J. *Nefertiti: Egypt's Sun Queen*, London, 1998

Velikovsky, I. *Oedipus and Akhnaton*, London, 1960

Weigall, A. *The Life and Times of Akhnaton, Pharaoh of Egypt*, London, 1922

4 The King and the Aten

Blackman, A.M. *A Study of the Liturgy Celebrated in the Temple of the Aton at El-Amarna*, in *Recueil d'Études Égyptologiques*, Paris, 1922, pp.505-527

Congdon, L.O. *The reliefs of Bek and Men at Aswan*, in AL, Volume Two, 1992, pp.42-49

Forbes, D.C. *The Akhenaten Colossi of Karnak: Their Discovery and Description*, in AL, Volume Three, 1994, pp.46-58

Watterson, B. *The House of Horus at Edfu: Ritual in an Ancient Egyptian Temple*, Stroud, 1998

5 Akhetaten — the Horizon of the Aten

Bierbrier, M. *The Tomb-builders of the Pharaohs*, London, 1982

Černy, J. 'The workmen of the king's tomb', in *Egypt from the death of Ramesses III to the end of the Twenty-first Dynasty*, CAH, vol.II:2, Chapter XXXV, 1975, pp.606-75

Kemp, B.J. *The Amarna Workmen's Village in Retrospect*, in JEA, 73, 1987, pp.21-50

Martin, G.T. *The Royal Tomb at el-'Amarna*. 2 vols. Pt 7 of The Rock Tombs of el-'Amarna, London, 1974, 1989

Romer, J. *Ancient Lives: the Story of the Pharaohs' Tombmakers*, London, 1984

Sandman, M. *Texts from the Time of Akhenaten*, Bibliotheca Aegyptiaca, 8, Brussels, 1938

6 Smenkhkare and the mystery of tomb 55

Davis, T.M. et al. *The Tomb of Queen Tiyi*. Reissued, with an Introduction and Bibliography by Nicholas Reeves, KMT Communications, San Francisco, 1990

Dodson, A. *Kings' Valley Tomb 55 and the Fates of the Amarna Kings*, in AL, Volume Three, 1994, pp.92-103

Fairman, H.W. *Once again the so-called coffin of Akhenaten*, in JEA, 47, 1961, pp.25-40

Forbes, D.C. *Tombs, Treasures, Mummies. Seven Great Discoveries of Egyptian Archaeology*,

Sebastopol, California, 1999

Gardiner, A. H. *The Graffito in the Tomb of Pere*, in JEA, 14, 1928, pp.10-11

Harrison, R.G. *An anatomical examination of the Pharaonic remains purported to be Akhenaten*, in JEA, 52, 1966, pp.95-119

Harrison, R.G., Connolly, R.C. and Abdalla, A. *Kinship of Smenkhkare and Tutankhamen affirmed by serological micromethod*, in Nature, 224 (25 October), 1969, pp.325-26

Hussien, F. and Harris, J.E. *The skeletal remains from Tomb No. 55*. Fifth International Congress of Egyptology, October 29 — November 3, Cairo 1988. Abstracts of papers, Cairo, 1988, pp.140-141

Ingals, B.K., et al. *The skull from Tomb No. 55*, Luxor. Fifth International Congress of Egyptology, October 29–November 3, Cairo 1988. Abstracts of papers, Cairo, 1988, p.142

Maspero, G. *New Light on Ancient Egypt*, 2nd ed., London, 1909, pp.291-98

Perepelkin, I.I. *Perevorot Amen-khotpa IV*, I/iii-iv, Moscow, 1967

Perepelkin, I.I. *Taina zolotogo groba*, Moscow, 1969. Translated by G. Perepelkin as *The Secret of the Gold Coffin*, Moscow, 1978

Reeves, C. N. *Valley of the Kings. The decline of a royal necropolis*, London, 1990

Roeder, G. *Amarna-Blocke aus Hermopolis*, Hildesheim, 1969

Smith, J.L. *Tomb, Temples and Ancient Art*, ed. Corinna Smith, Norman, Oklahoma 1956, pp.54-75

7 The aftermath of the Amarna Age

Bennett, J. *The Restoration Inscription of Tutankhamun*, in JEA, 25,1939, p.8 foll.

Brier, R. *The Murder of Tutankhamun*, London, 1998

Carter, H. *The Tomb of Tutankhamen*, London, 1972

Carter, H. and A. Mace. *The Tomb of Tutankhamen*, Vols I-III, London, 1923–33

Černy, J. *Hieratic Inscriptions from the Tomb of Tutankhamun*, Oxford, 1952

Harrison, R.G. *Post mortem on two pharaohs:Was Tutankhamun's skull fractured?* in *Buried History*, 1972, pp.18-24

Harrison, R.G. *Tutankhamun's postmortem*, in The Lancet, 1973, p.259

Harrison, R.G. and A.G. Abdalla. *The remains of Tutankhamun*, in *Antiquity*, 46, 1972, pp.8-14

Harrison, R.G., et al. *A mummified foetus from the tomb of Tutankhamun*, in *Antiquity*, 53, 1979, pp.19-21

Forbes, D.C. *A New Hypothesis for Tutankhamen's Early Demise*, in KMT, 3 (1), 1992, p.61

Hayes, W.C. *Inscriptions from the Palace of Amenophis III*, in JNES, 10, 1951, pp. 35-36, 82-111, 231-242

Martin, G.T. *The Hidden Tombs of Memphis: New Discoveries from the Time of Tutankhamun and Ramesses the Great*, London, 1991

Reeves, N. *The Complete Tutankhamun*, London, 1990

8 The uncovering of Amarna

Arnold, D. 'The workshop of the sculptor Thutmose', in *The Royal Women of Amarna: Images of Beauty from Ancient Egypt*, New York, 1996, pp.41-84

Davies, N. de G. *The Rock Tombs of El-Amarna*, I-VI, London, 1903–1908

Davies, N. de G. 'Mural Paintings in the City of Akhetaten', in JEA, 7, 1921, pp.1-7

Davies, N. de G. 'The Paintings of the Northern Palace', in H. Frankfort, ed., *The Mural Paintings of el-'Amarneh*, London, 1929, pp.58-71

Drower, M.S. *Flinders Petrie: A Life in Archaeology*, London, 1985

Flynn, S.J.A. *Sir John Gardiner Wilkinson: Traveller and Egyptologist 1797–1875*, Oxford, 1997

James, T.G.H., ed. *Excavating in Egypt: The Egypt Exploration Society 1882–1982*, Chapter 5 (El-Amarna), London, 1982

Krauss, R. 'Der Bildhauer Thutmose in Amarna' in *Jahrbuch Preussischer Kulturbesitz*, 20, 1983, pp.119-32

Martin, G.T. *The Royal Tomb at El-Amarna*, 2 vols, London, 1974, 1989

Moran, W.J. *The Amarna Letters*, Baltimore, 1992

Peet, T.E., Woolley, C.L., Frankfort, H., Pendlebury, J.D.S., et al. *The City of Akhenaten*, Parts I-III, London, 1961

Pendlebury, J.D.S. *Tell el-Amarna*, London, 1935

Petrie, W.M.F. *Tell el-Amarna*, London, 1894

and some novels of interest:

Drury, Allen. *A God Against the Gods*, London, 1976

Fraser, Helen. *Fulfilment at Noon*, London, 1950

Hamilton, Alexandra. *The Beautiful One*, London, 1979

— *The Lady of Grace*, London, 1979

— *The Devious Being*, London, 1980

Mailer, Norman. *Ancient Evenings*, London, 1997

Smith, Wilbur. *River God*, London, 1994

References

[1] Known to the Greeks as Xois.

[2] Inebhedj (City of the White Wall) is often referred to as Memphis, the name by which the ancient Greeks knew it.

[3] Hansen, 1994.

[4] ARE, II, 478.

[5] Tell Nebi Mend, some 18 miles (30 km) south-west of Homs.

[6] Biblical Armageddon, 90 miles (150 km) north of Gaza.

[7] Erman, 1966, pp.167-69.

[8] The campaigns are recorded in the Annals carved on walls in the Temple of Amun at Karnak (Luxor). For translations, see ANET, p.234 foll.

[9] The Iliad, Book 9; translated by Alexander Pope, The World's Classics, Oxford University Press, page 176-77.

[10] ARE, II, 12, 37-8.

[11] Today called the Valley of the Tombs of the Kings, or the Valley of the Kings. The tombs in it have been allotted numbers in order of discovery in modern times and are often referred to as KV (Kings' Valley) followed by the appropriate number.

[12] Bryan, 1991, pp. 108-120.

[13] Kitchen, 1962, p.24, n.2.

[14] A cubit was based on the length of a forearm (18 — 22 inches). Using the lower figure, Tiye's basin was some 1708m long (over a mile) by some 323m wide.

[15] Nos 29 and 28 in Knudtzon, 1907–15.

[16] Partridge, 1994, pp.85-86.

[17] Reeves & Wilkinson, 1996, pp.110-115.

[18] Sethe & Helck, 1906–58, p.1648, lines 9-11.

[19] Strabo, Geography, 17.1.46 (Loeb Classical Library).

[20] Johnson, 1990.

[21] Theban necropolis tomb numbers 55, 57, 192 and 48 respectively.

[22] Reeves & Wilkinson, op. cit., p.174-178.

[23] Johnson, 1996.

[24] Harris, 1990; Forbes, 1999.

[25] *Akhnaten*: An Opera in Three Acts by Philip Glass, first performed in 1984.

[26] Breasted, 1924, p.127.

[27] Velikovsky, 1960.

[28] For a summary of the evidence for and against a co-regency see KMT, 2 (2), 1991, p.64 foll.

29 Aldred, 1988, pp.221-222.

30 Aldred, 1968, Chapter 6.

31 Johnson, 1991.

32 Today called El-Ashmunein; known to the ancient Greeks as Hermopolis Magna because they identified Thoth, the city's chief deity, with Hermes, messenger of the Greek gods.

33 Smith & Redford, 1976, Pls 19, 28-33.

34 *op. cit.*, Pls 32, 33.

35 Hayes, 1959, p.294.

36 Fairman, 1961.

37 Reeves, 1988.

38 Roeder, 1969, Pl.10, 826 VIII A..

39 No. K27 in Knudtzon, 1907–15.

40 Harris et al., 1978.

41 Martin, 1989.

42 Dodson, 1990.

43 Aldred, 1988, p.285.

44 Harris, 1974; Allen, 1991; Murnane, 1995, pp.10, 205-8.

45 Gardiner, 1928.

46 Allen, 1991, p.85, n.56.

47 No.51: obverse in Knudtzon, *op. cit.*

48 Moran, 1992.

49 No. 162: 36-41 in Knudtzon, *op. cit.*

50 Ibid, Nos. 164-170.

51 BM No. 65800.

52 Meaning: 'Beautiful are the Forms of Re, The Unique One Who Belongs to Re', *i.e.* Akhenaten.

53 Translation by Barbara Watterson.

54 From the Book of Psalms in the King James version of the Bible.

55 Watterson, 1998, p.75 foll.

56 Now in Rome: the obelisk was dedicated to Thutmose III but finished and erected by Thutmose IV.

57 Parts of 15 statues were recovered during Chevrier's 1926 excavations; see Forbes, 1994.

58 A claim found in a *graffito* at Aswan. See Congdon, 1992.

59 Sandman, 1938, pp. 119-131.

60 Kemp, 1987.

61 Bierbrier, 19

62 Peet *et al*, 1923, pp 51-91 (village) and 92-108 (chapels).

63 No. 525.

64 Most of the surviving pieces of the sarcophagus are now in the garden of the Egyptian Museum in Cairo where an attempt has been made to reassemble them.

65 All the pieces here discussed are now in the Ägypisches Museum in Berlin with the exception of two of the heads of princesses, which are in the Egyptian Museum in Cairo.

66 Gardiner, 1928.
67 Roeder, 1969.
68 Reeves, 1990, pp.42-49, 55-60.
69 Now in Cairo Museum along with most of the other objects found in the tomb.
70 Smith, 1956.
71 Davis, 1910, p.15.
72 *ibid.*, p.11.
73 For a history of debate up to the late 1980s, and an exhaustive bibliography on the subject, by Nicholas Reeves *see* Davis 1990, iv-xiv and xv-1.
74 Dodson, 1994, p.94 (caption to picture).
75 Perepelkin, 1967, pp.114-148.
76 Fairman, 1961.
77 Harrison *et al*, 1969.
78 Harrison, 1966.
79 Hussien and Harris, 1988.
80 Hayes, 1951.
81 Černy, 1952, no.25.
82 Translation by Watterson. For a translation of the complete text *see* Bennett, 1939.
83 Martin, 1991, pp.147-188.
84 *op. cit.*, pp.35-98.
85 Numbered Th 40, located at Qurnet Murai on the west bank at Luxor.
86 Nos 9 and 10 in Knudtzon, 1907–15: *see* Bibliography to Chapter 2.
87 Brier, 1998.
88 Forbes, 1992.
89 Carter, 1923–33, Vol. III, pp.63-64.
90 The present whereabouts of the foetus is unknown; the premature child is in Cairo University School of Medicine.
91 Harrison, 1979.
92 Translated in ANET, p.319.
93 Martin, 1991, pp.97-98.
94 Told to the author by the late Professor H.W. Fairman.
95 Baikie, 1926, p.3.
96 What is left of the floor, heavily restored, is now in the Egyptian Museum in Cairo.
97 Now in the Ashmolean Museum, Oxford.
98 Pendlebury, 1935, p.xix.
99 James, 1982, p.95.
100 Krauss, 1983.
101 Arnold, 1996.
102 Frankfort. H., ed. *The Mural Paintings of El-'Amarneh*, London 1929.
103 Now in the British Museum.
104 In JEA, 21, 1935, pp.129-30.
105 Martin, 1974, 1989.

General Index

Index of Ancient Egyptian Words